Management for Professionals

The Springer series Management for Professionals comprises high-level business and management books for executives. The authors are experienced business professionals and renowned professors who combine scientific background, best practice, and entrepreneurial vision to provide powerful insights into how to achieve business excellence.

More information about this series at http://www.springer.com/series/10101

Sen Sendjaya

Personal and Organizational Excellence through Servant Leadership

Learning to Serve, Serving to Lead, Leading to Transform

 Springer

Sen Sendjaya
Department of Management
Monash University
Caulfield East
VIC, Australia

ISSN 2192-8096   ISSN 2192-810X   (electronic)
Management for Professionals
ISBN 978-3-319-16195-2   ISBN 978-3-319-16196-9   (eBook)
DOI 10.1007/978-3-319-16196-9

Library of Congress Control Number: 2015936032

Springer Cham Heidelberg New York Dordrecht London

Printed on acid-free paper

Springer International Publishing AG Switzerland is part of Springer Science+Business Media (www.
springer.com)

To my wife, Dr Lyfie Sugianto, and children, Tiffany and Calvin. Thanks for your grace and patience as I fumble my way towards becoming a servant leader.

Contents

Introduction to Servant Leadership

In a world preoccupied by self-interest and meticulously designed to make us function in a perpetual rat race, servant leadership with its seemingly lofty appeal is often met with a suspicion and cynicism. Like a strange voice in the wilderness, it is visibly distinct from other leadership approaches because of its deliberate choice to put other people's needs and aspirations above one's own. Servant leaders make conscious decisions daily to use their talents for the growth of individual followers first, the organization second, and their own last. That is probably why it gains currency in many organizations operating in the post-Enron world. Today that strange voice in the wilderness has become a much more familiar and stronger voice in the organization.

1.1 Working Definition

Scientific research studies over the past decade have shown that servant leadership is an intellectually compelling and emotionally satisfying theory of leadership with relevance and application to the workplace settings. On the basis on my research, teaching, and consulting experience, I have developed a working definition of servant leadership as follows.

> Servant leadership is a holistic approach to leadership that engages both leaders and followers through its (1) service orientation, (2) authenticity focus, (3) relational emphasis, (4) moral courage, (5) spiritual motivation, and (6) transforming influence such that they are both transformed into what they are capable of becoming.

The following paragraphs briefly unpack the definition and highlight a few points that will be further elaborated in subsequent chapters. First, servant leadership is a leadership approach that reflects an internal orientation of the heart to serve others. It stems from a conviction of the heart to transform other people into the best versions of themselves with moral courage and spiritual insights. It does not

© Springer International Publishing Switzerland 2015
S. Sendjaya, *Personal and Organizational Excellence through Servant Leadership*, Management for Professionals, DOI 10.1007/978-3-319-16196-9_1

originate therefore from the leader's competency, but a strong desire within the leader to help others to be what they are capable of becoming. This desire is significantly enhanced by leadership roles where power and influence are used in the most positive ways. In short, servanthood comes before leadership. It speaks of someone with a servant's heart who leads. The curious juxtaposition between servanthood and leadership is not a semantics issue. It serves to highlight a profound understanding of what it really means to lead.

No wonder servant leadership is typically understood in reference to its emphasis on other people (Greenleaf 1977, p. 13): "The servant leader is a servant first . . . It begins with the natural feeling that one wants to serve, to serve first. Then conscious choice brings one to aspire to lead." It is important to note that servant leadership does not operate out of weakness, inferiority, or a lack of self-respect. Only those with a secure sense of self, strength of character, and psychological maturity are willing and able to serve others through their leadership. As such, being a servant leader is not about being courteous or friendly. It undertakes commitment to make personal sacrifices to develop others to their maximum potential.

Second, it is a follower-centered approach to leadership. The focus is not the leader or even the organization, but the relationship between leaders and followers which engages both the leaders and followers, and brings the most benefits to the followers. In servant leadership relationships, therefore, the leaders act as stewards – they consider their followers as people who have been entrusted to them to be elevated to their better selves and to be what they are capable of becoming. Followers tend to respond well to servant leaders because they have proven themselves trustworthy as servants.

The hallmark of servant leaders, therefore, is their deliberate choice to serve others. In the words of Daft and Lengel (2000, p. 176):

> The desire to serve others takes precedence over the desire to be in a formal leadership position. Such individuals move into leadership through service rather than from the need to exercise power and control. Servant leaders make a conscious choice to use their gifts in the cause of change and growth for individuals and the organization.

The success story of Starbucks whose culture resolves around prioritizing employees' needs and aspirations is one of many that captures this very principle. In the words of a former Starbucks executive: "We're in the people business serving coffee, not the coffee business serving people" (Behar and Goldstein 2007, p. xv).

Third, it is a holistic approach to leadership. My research thus far has repeatedly confirmed that there are six empirically and conceptually distinct dimensions of servant leadership: service (*Voluntary Subordination*), authenticity (*Authentic Self*), relationship (*Covenantal Relationship*), morality (*Responsible Morality*), spirituality (*Transcendental Spirituality*), and transformation (*Transforming Influence*). Because servant leadership is multidimensional, the rational, relational, ethical, emotional, and spiritual sides of followers and leaders are equally cared for in the leadership process. This holistic emphasis enables servant leadership to produce sustained and desirable outcomes in organizations.

Fourth, it has a developmental emphasis, seeking to make positive differences in others. Servant leaders empower followers to "grow healthier, wiser, freer, more autonomous, and more likely themselves to become servants" (Greenleaf 1977, pp. 13–14). As an other-orientated rather than leader-centered leadership approach, the effectiveness of the servant leadership approach is therefore measured by the change and growth experienced primarily by followers.

Since leadership is more 'caught' than 'taught', followers themselves will be transformed into servant leaders. The transformational effects in followers is achieved through what is often perceived as a counterintuitive way, that is servant leaders willingly sacrificing their needs and wants in order to serve others, instead of serving their own selves by sacrificing other people. In fact, the moral and spiritual ideals of servant leadership guard servant leaders from the oft-cited leadership temptation to manipulate followers, making servant leadership a distinct approach to leadership.

1.2   Rationale for Servant Leadership

Having spent the best years of my adult life working in academia on the subject of leadership, I have experienced first-hand and observed two widespread phenomena when it comes to leadership practice. First, many leadership models proposed by leadership 'consultants' of all shapes and size make a lot a common sense but are scientifically suspect. That is, they are not based on rigorous scientific studies that would ensure their validity and reliability. For example, the techniques or tools that are purported to measure and improve a certain set of behaviors may not accurately capture the behaviors in question (i.e., lacking validity) or a leadership practice that works well in one company may not work in others (i.e. lacking reliability).

The second phenomenon is exactly the contrary. Endless leadership theories that have gone through rigorous validation studies have little relevance to the real-world practice. These leadership studies are reported in technical journals read mainly by academics and their doctorate students (often they read them not because they want to, but they have to). Granted these studies are based on sound methodologies, but findings of these studies often do not get translated into actionable corporate practices for various reasons. A colleague at McKinsey Consulting echoes that sentiment in his remark during a conversation: "University research is too naïve, too complex, and too slow."

Why then do we need another theory of leadership, or another book for that matter? And why servant leadership? These are fair questions that demand a satisfactory answer, and ones that I intend to address upfront in this introductory chapter. As delineated in the following paragraphs, there are five reasons why servant leadership can be a foundation for personal and organizational excellence – contextual, anecdotal, empirical, philosophical, and cross-cultural.

1.2.1 Contextual

The need for servant leadership cannot be overstated against the backdrop of destructive leadership in organizations and the severity of its damages to both individuals and organizations. Endless high profile scandals involving corporate leaders in the global arena continue make headline news. The severity and perpetuity of the damages both to individual and organizations caused by destructive leaders are well documented. The negative effects of destructive leadership have been identified including job tension, emotional fatigue, deviant behavior, bullying, alienation, abuse of power, and so on (Sendjaya et al. 2008). Abusive supervision in the US alone, for example, has been estimated to cost nearly $24 billion annually associated with employee turnover, absenteeism, lawsuits, etc. (Tepper 2007). An overwhelming majority of the bullying cases, identified a superior as the alleged bully. As a moral-laden and other-orientated leadership approach, servant leadership has been shown to bring about significant changes in the opposite direction. For example, it facilitates moral dialogue between leaders and followers, ensuring that both the ends they seek and the means they employ are morally legitimized, thoughtfully reasoned, and ethically justified (Sendjaya et al. 2008).

What transpires from the recent failures of leaders and collapse of organizations across the globe is the limitation of performance-oriented leadership approaches that sacrifice people on the altar of profit and growth. The unprecedented challenges that confront contemporary leaders today cannot be met with leadership approaches that regard people merely as units of production or expendable resources in a profit and loss statement. While such approaches may bring about impressive growth and 'performance beyond expectations', these results are not sustainable in the long run as the relational, ethical, emotional, and spiritual sides of followers and, to a lesser extent, leaders are neglected.

Against such backdrop, servant leadership has attracted a surge of scholarly interest. It is a holistic and value-laden leadership model that empowers people to be both effective and ethical. While often underrated, the relevance and currency of servant leadership relative to other leadership models in today's context are quite obvious.

1.2.2 Anecdotal

The steady increase of anecdotal evidences of servant leadership practices in high performing companies such as Starbucks, Southwest Airlines, Ritz-Carlton, ServiceMaster are often reported in the popular press (Gergen 2006). While these corporate practices can be downplayed as isolated cases, as critics may suggest, servant leadership has spurred curiosity beyond the capacity of scholars to keep pace either theoretically or empirically. Most research into new leadership models or approaches struggle to find corporate examples or scenarios to which the models or theories can fit. Often the researchers have to disseminate the new idea, convince the key decision makers, and train or coach the leaders to apply the leadership approach. Such is not the case with servant leadership.

The late Bernard Bass, a prominent leadership researcher, affirmed the importance of servant leadership for future organizational leaders: "The strength of the servant leadership movement and its many links to encouraging follower learning, growth, and autonomy, suggests that the untested theory will play a role in the future leadership of the learning organization" (2000, p. 33). The increasing importance of transparency, accountability, humility, compassion, and other values vital to human flourishing in today's contemporary organizations provide the impetus for servant leadership to take root in the corporate context.

Fortune's annual survey of "Top 100 Best Companies to Work For in America" consistently includes winners that advocate the philosophy of servant leadership. This implies that if you work for one of the best employers, there is a high probability servant leadership is implemented as an organization-wide practice. These terrific employers come in various sizes, employing anywhere between 1,000 and 167,000 employees. In addition to the aforementioned Starbucks, Southwest Airlines, Ritz-Carlton, ServiceMaster, the list includes companies like TDIndustries, SAS, Zappos.com, Container Store, Intel, Marriott, Nordstorm, and Synovus Financial.

While these servant leadership-infused firms might represent an anomaly in the larger corporate context of that worships the bottom line over other things, they are like stars that shine the brightest in a dark sky. What Peter Drucker, the father of modern management, once observed is in line with the servant leadership philosophy, "Profit is to a corporation what oxygen is for the human body; necessary for its existence, but not the reason for it." Servant leadership offers a fresh leadership framework around which organizations can build positive work environments that treats profit as a necessary means rather than *the* reason for existence.

Jack Lowe (1998), CEO and Chairman of TDIndustries, which is one of the largest mechanical contractors in America, wrote that TDIndustries has employed servant leadership as an organizational-wide leadership development philosophy and program. He believes that when people become grounded in servant leadership, trust grows and the foundation for organizational excellence is established. The culture of trust is evident in the ownership of TDIndustries by the employees (30 top managers and the founder's widow own 25 % of the stock; lower-level employees own the rest), which explains why the company's 1,273 employees are called partners.

In a similar vein, Synovus Financial Corporation, a multi-billion dollar financial services firm, illustrates the servant leadership concept through a strong commitment to family-oriented policies such as work flexibility, leave for new parents, work/life balance, and advancing women in their careers. Chairman and CEO Jimmy Blanchard outlines the company's values in the following way: "The heart of the servant-leader brings order, brings meaning to employees. When employees feel order and meaning and that they are a part of a team that stands for something good, that there is a higher calling than just working to get a paycheck, that they are improving mankind, there is an energy level that explodes and great things happen" (Chappel 2000, p. 5).

Under the leadership of founder and CEO Herb Kelleher, Southwest Airlines had one of the most distinguished organizational cultures in America. The company has been recognized as one of the most admired companies in the world and the most admired airline in the world year after year. Servant leadership principles provide the foundation for altruism, defined as the constructive, gratifying service to others, and one of the core values of Southwest's culture (Quick 1992). Quick (1992) noted that employees of Southwest are notable for their caring approach and appreciation of each other, as well as in the service of others.

Many organizational leaders see themselves as servant leaders today. William Pollard, Chairman of The ServiceMaster, is a case in point. His company has been recognized by *Fortune* magazine as the best service company among the *Fortune* 500 firms. Describing himself as, and encouraging others to be, leaders who lead with a servant's heart, Pollard (1997, pp. 49–50) contended that the real leader is not the "person with the most distinguished title, the highest pay, or the longest tenure . . . but the role model, the risk taker, the servant; not the person who promotes himself or herself, but the promoter of others."

1.2.3   Empirical

In the past the lack of empirical evidence has been cited as the primary reason behind the sluggish reception of the servant leadership construct. The last decade however has seen a significant positive change with multiple rigorous studies on servant leadership appearing in top ranking academic journals in the field such as *Academy of Management Journal, Journal of Applied Psychology, Journal of Management, Leadership Quarterly, Personnel Psychology,* and *Journal of Management Studies.*

Research evidence unequivocally shows that servant leadership is a better predictor than transformational leadership – perhaps the most popular and researched leadership theory to date – in relation to a few key outcome variables. Relative to transformational leadership, servant leadership explains additional variance on team performance (10 %) (Schaubroeck et al. 2011), employee satisfaction (11 %), commitment (7 %) and intention to stay (11 %) (Schneider and George 2011), organizational citizenship behavior (19 %) and in-role performance (5 %) (Liden et al. 2008), and firm performance (28 %) (Peterson et al. 2012). These studies confirm the reliability and validity of servant leadership to be applied in the corporate context.

1.2.4   Philosophical

The philosophical basis of servant leadership serves to answer *who* the leader is (self-concept), *why* the leader does leadership (service orientation) and *how* the leader does leadership (standard operating procedure).

Self-Concept Since 1980s leadership scholars have resurrected the myth of leaders as isolated heroes controlling and commanding organizations from on high. When they use the word leaders, the pictures they have in mind are of those people at the top of an organizational pyramid. The rest are the followers who take orders from them. Stripped to the bare minimum, much that has been written in the leadership literature essentially represent a recurrence of the great man theory in the 1960s.

In contrast, servant leaders first view themselves as stewards. The word "stewardship" is derived from the Greek word 'oikonomia'. The original meaning of the word is rooted in the idea of a house manager. The 'oikonomos', which is translated steward, was entrusted with the responsibility of managing the business affairs of a household. The word often referred to a servant who was given responsibility over money, property, goods or other servants. In our current terminology, the word carries the idea of a trustee, one to whom something of value is entrusted. Block (1993) asserts that the concept of stewardship essentially is the willingness to be accountable for the well-being of the larger community by operating in the service of those around us. However, Block (1993) views stewardship and leadership as mutually exclusive concepts because unlike leadership stewardship cannot accommodate both accountability and control together. Citing the case of earth stewardship, Block maintains that "there needs to be a way for me to be accountable for the earth without having to control it" (1993, pp. 18–19). This is where my view is different from his – no doubt the premise he employs might is right, but the conclusion is not.

Rather than taking a limited view of leadership, I concur with Senge's (1990) delineation that, when leaders serve others there is a sense of stewardship within them that is evident on two distinct levels: stewardship for the people whom they lead, and stewardship for the larger purpose or mission on which the organization is built. The operative word in the latter part is 'larger', which refers to a more fundamental set of corporate objectives rather than just the bottom lines. As stewards, servant leaders regard their followers as people who have been entrusted to them to be elevated to their better selves. Thus, the leader-follower relationship is that of a client-server relationship as opposed to a master-slave relationship.

Service Orientation Contrary to a somewhat utopian view that leadership should be abandoned, authoritative leadership is still essential in organizations. No doubt we have seen repeated cases of the abuse of leadership. When we witness people jockeying for position and clamoring for status and using their power to put others in a covert bondage, we are tempted to throw up our hands and try to do away with leadership altogether. But think about the alternative scenario. An infantile anarchy is no better than an oppressive dictatorship. The solution to this dilemma is to embrace a concept of servant leadership whose service orientation is something outside the leader, namely the followers.

In contrast to other leadership approaches in general, servant leadership focuses more on followers and their development than on organizations and their objectives.

For example, a transformational leader will excite and inspire followers to go beyond the call of duty, but these behaviors are typically motivated by a preoccupation with the organizational goals rather than followers' development. On the contrary, servant leaders are genuinely focused on promoting others' interest over and above those of the leader or leader-defined organizational interests as well as promoting a sense of community amongst team members and fairness in the work context (Sendjaya et al. 2008). As servant leaders both place the good of those led over self-interest displaying a sustained and altruistic commitment to help followers to grow (Giampetro-Meyer et al. 1998), their influence and authority becomes means to serve others to be what they are capable of becoming.

De Pree (1989, p. 12), a former Chairman and CEO of Herman Miller, wrote in his insightful book *Leadership Is An Art,* that "The signs of outstanding leadership appear primarily among the followers. Are the followers reaching their potential? Are they learning? Serving?". This does not necessarily mean that the organization's goals are left unattended since the two goals of serving followers and serving the organization are not mutually exclusive. The focus, however, is on the former; the latter is the by-product of the former. As servant leaders keep their priorities on the followers, they constantly ask themselves whether they truly build people, or build their personal ambitions (often embedded in the organization's objectives) and use people to achieve them.

Standard Operating Procedure Ciulla (1995) maintains that for leadership to be effective, it has to include both technical competencies and moral capacities. It is insufficient for leaders to be effective but unethical. Unfortunately, cases of technically capable but morally disappointing corporate leaders abound. The more corrupt they are, the greater our yearning for morally sound or ethical leaders. Sergiovanni (1992) describes moral-laden leadership as a new kind of leadership practice that is rooted in moral authority. The greatest battle cry of leadership today is the need for, to use Burns' (1978, p. 452) phrase, "moral, uplifting, transcending leadership."

I develop my theorizing of the moral component of servant leadership on the basis of Burns' (1978) transforming leadership and Greenleaf's (1977) servant leadership conceptualizations. Burns bases his theory on two pressing moral issues; the morality of the means and ends, and the public and private morality of a leader. In addition, his notion of transforming leaders is focused on those who appeal to positive moral values and higher-order needs of followers. As such, Burns' transforming leaders are identical to Greenleaf's servant leaders who " . . . seek to raise the consciousness of followers by appealing to higher ideals and moral values such as liberty, justice, equality, peace, justice, peace, and humanitarianism, not to baser emotions such as fear, greed, jealousy, or hatred" (Yukl 1990, p. 210). Servant leaders themselves are moral agents who seek to engage in moral actions and their followers, while being served, are transformed into moral agents and eventually, servant leaders themselves.

1.2.5 Cross-Cultural

The reason why it is important to examine the generalizability of servant leadership, or any other leadership theories for that matter, is twofold. First, according to the Global Leadership and Organizational Behavior Effectiveness (GLOBE) project which still stands as the most comprehensive cross-national leadership study involving over 60 countries, there exists perceptions of leadership effectiveness in each society (House et al. 2004). Consequently effective leadership necessitates a good understanding of the local culture in which leaders operate and their adaptive capacity to each local culture (House et al. 2002, 2004).

Second, most leadership theories originate from the West in particular North America. Servant leadership was not an exception, it was primarily studied in the West and practiced by American companies. The Western style of leadership might be developed on assumptions which are partially or entirely irrelevant to other parts of the world (Pellegrini and Scandura 2008). Researchers have concurred that leadership approaches that are effective in Western countries may be inappropriate in other cultures (Blunt and Jones 1997; Shahin and Wright 2004) or even counterproductive (Beyer 1999).

Is servant leadership relevant in non-US countries? From research perspective, preliminary empirical evidence from cross-cultural studies seem to suggest that it is relevant but not without some qualifications (Hale and Fields 2007; Mittal and Dorfman 2012; Washington et al. 2006; West and Bocarnea 2008). A study found that African Americans leaders exhibited more servant leadership behaviors in comparison to 'white leaders' in the U.S. (Washington et al. 2006). This finding was somewhat expected since African Americans are strongly predisposed to kinship relationships that extend to the entire African American community and hence highly value cooperation and interdependence. Another study exploring servant leadership in Ghana and the U.S. found that the servant leadership values of integrity, humility, and accountability might be incompatible with the social norms that accept hierarchies and inequalities in Ghana.

Yet another study showed that servant leadership was practiced and accepted in both Australia and Indonesia but its practice would be moderated by culture (Pekerti and Sendjaya 2010). Australian leaders exhibited more behaviors associated with authenticity, while Indonesian leaders exhibited more behavior associated with morality and influence. No significant difference reported between Australian and Indonesian leaders behaviors associated with service, relational, and spirituality dimensions. These findings might be attributable to culture-specific differences in terms of societal profile and cultural identities of the two countries.

Finally the latest investigation of the generalizability of servant leadership was conducted using the GLOBE data. Mittal and Dorfman (2012) reported that servant leadership is perceived differently in the West and East. The emphatic and humble sides of servant leaders will be more positively valued in the Southern Asian cultures than European cultures. On the contrary, the European endorses highly the egalitarian and empowering emphasis of servant leaders.

As for its implementation in Asia, given the speculative concern that servant leaders are 'weak' leaders, having leaders with a serving orientation might be counterintuitive in the Asian high power distance context where followers idolize leaders and perceive them as 'strong' figures. However, recent studies provide more evidence that servant leadership does positively contribute to the more effective functioning of the organization in Asia (Yoshida et al. 2014).

In summary, while cultures shape one's perceptions of servant leadership, it can be applied in various cultures and has been applied by practitioners at different levels of organizations in multiple nations.

While servant leadership is not a panacea to the global epidemic of toxic leadership, an appreciation of the philosophy and spirit of servant leadership will help leaders and followers relate with each other in more ethical and meaningful ways. This book provides an evidence-based actionable framework and measure of servant leadership to assist management practitioners build effective and ethical workplaces. The following chapters highlight its unique contributions to the study of leadership and the practice of corporate and individual leadership. Understanding the reasons why highly successful employers apply servant leadership will assist leaders and managers to reflect on, challenge, and hone their leadership approach in inspiring people to excellence and building positive work environments.

To set the context Chap. 2 summarizes key research studies on servant leadership comprising the origin of the concept, theoretical and empirical distinctions between servant leadership and select leadership theories, outcomes of servant leadership, development of the 35-item Servant Leadership Behavior Scale (SLBS), and common objections to servant leadership. The six empirically tested dimensions of servant leadership (*Voluntary Subordination, Authentic Self, Covenantal Relationship, Responsible Morality, Transcendental Spirituality,* and *Transforming Influence*), which emerge out of my research conducted over more than a decade in the Western and Eastern contexts, are outlined in Chaps. 3, 4, 5, 6, 7, 8. In each of those chapters, select comments from senior executives in Australian for-profit and not-for-profit organizations who participated in the semi-structured interviews I conducted will be featured to illustrate key points. Information on the methods used in the interview process is provided in the Appendix. Each of the six chapters concludes with a set of servant leadership commitments that correspond to the servant leadership dimensions. Finally, the concluding chapter offers a framework for servant leadership development.

In summary, this book outlines the multidimensional servant leadership behavior. Leaders can adapt the psychometrically valid measurement instrument (SLBS) for leadership assessment, selection, and training purposes, and develop strategies to leverage the six behavioral dimensions of servant leadership at the personal, team, and organizational level. Table 1.1 shows the servant leadership dimensions, values, and commitments – think of it as a roadmap for the book. The 35 actionable commitments of servant leadership are mapped onto their corresponding values and dimensions. These commitments are identical to the SLBS, hence can be used with confidence by leadership practitioners across cultures.

Table 1.1 Dimensions, values, and commitments of servant leadership

Dimensions	Values	Commitments
Voluntary Subordination	Being A Servant	1. Consider others' needs and interests above my own
	Acts of Service	2. Use power in service to others, not for my own ambition
		3. Be more conscious of my responsibilities than my rights
		4. Serve others with no regards of backgrounds (gender, race, etc)
		5. Demonstrate that I care through sincere, practical deeds
		6. Listen to others with intent to understand
		7. Assist others without seeking acknowledgement or compensation
Authentic Self	Humility	8. Avoid being defensive when confronted
	Integrity	9. When criticized focus on the message not the messenger
	Accountability	10. Practice what I preach
	Security	11. Give others the right to question my actions and decisions
	Vulnerability	12. Let others take control of situations when appropriate
		13. Be willing to say "I was wrong" to others
Covenantal Relationship	Acceptance	14. Affirm my trust in others
	Availability	15. Accept others as they are, irrespective of their failures
	Equality	16. Respect others for who they are, not how they make me feel
	Collaboration	17. Spend time to build a professional relationship with others
		18. Treat people as equal partners
		19. Have confidence in others, even when the risk seems great
Responsible Morality	Moral Reasoning	20. Take a resolute stand on moral principles
	Moral Action	21. Encourage others to engage in moral reasoning
		22. Enhance others' capacity for moral actions
		23. Employ morally justified means to achieve legitimate ends
		24. Emphasize on doing what is right rather than looking good
Transcendental Spirituality	Transcendental Beliefs	25. Am driven by a sense of a higher calling
	Interconnectedness	26. Help others to generate a sense of meaning out of everyday life
	Sense of Mission	27. Help others to find a clarity of purpose and direction
	Wholeness	28. Promote values that transcend self-interest and material success
Transforming Influence	Vision	29. Articulate a shared vision to give inspiration and meaning
	Empowerment	30. Minimize barriers that inhibit others' success
	Modeling	31. Contribute to others' personal and professional growth
	Mentoring	32. Lead by personal example
	Trust	33. Inspire others to lead by serving
		34. Draw the best out of others
		35. Allow others to experiment and be creative without fear

References

Bass, B. M. (2000). The future of leadership in learning organizations. *Journal of Leadership Studies, 7*(3), 18–40.

Behar, H., & Goldstein, J. (2007). *It's not about the coffee: Lessons on putting people first from a life at starbucks*. New York: Penguin.

Beyer, J. M. (1999). Taming and promoting charisma to change organizations. *Leadership Quarterly, 10*(2), 307–330.

Block, P. (1993). *Stewardship: Choosing service over self-interest*. San Francisco: Berrett Koehler.

Blunt, P., & Jones, M. L. (1997). Exploring the limits of western leadership theory in East Asia and Africa. *Personnel Review, 26*(1/2), 6–23.

Burns, J. M. (1978). *Leadership*. New York: Harper & Row.

Chappel, D. (2000). Fortune's "best companies to work for" embrace servant leadership. *The Servant Leader*, Spring.

Ciulla, J. B. (1995). Leadership ethics: Mapping the territory. *Business Ethics Quarterly, 5*(1), 5–25.

Daft, R. L., & Lengel, R. H. (2000). *Fusion leadership: Unlocking the subtle forces that change people and organizations*. San Francisco: Berrett-Koehler.

De Pree, M. (1989). *Leadership is an art*. New York: Dell Publishing.

Gergen, D. (2006, June 11). Bad news for bullies. *U.S. News and World Report, 140*, 54.

Giampetro-Meyer, A., Brown, T., Browne, M. N., & Kubasek, N. (1998). Do we really want more leaders in business? *Journal of Business Ethics, 17*(15), 1727–1736.

Greenleaf, R. K. (1977). *Servant leadership*. Mahwah: Paulist Press.

Hale, J. R., & Fields, D. L. (2007). Exploring servant leadership across cultures: A study of followers in Ghana and the USA. *Leadership, 3*(4), 397–417.

House, R. J., Hanges, P. J., Javidan, M., & Dorfman, P. W. (2002). Understanding cultures and implicit leadership theories across the globe: An introduction to project GLOBE. *Journal of World Business, 37*(1), 3–10.

House, R. J., Hanges, P. J., Javidan, M., Dorfman, P. W., & Gupta, V. (2004). *Leadership, culture, and organizations: The GLOBE study of 62 societies*. Beverly Hills: Sage.

Liden, R. C., Wayne, S. J., Zhao, H., & Henderson, D. (2008). Servant leadership: Development of a multidimensional measure and multi-level assessment. *The Leadership Quarterly, 19*(2), 161–177.

Lowe, J. (1998). Trust: The invaluable asset. In L. C. Spears (Ed.), *Insights on leadership*. New York: Wiley.

Mittal, R., & Dorfman, P. W. (2012). Servant leadership across cultures. *Journal of World Business, 47*(4), 555–570.

Pekerti, A., & Sendjaya, S. (2010). Exploring servant leadership across cultures: Comparative study in Australia and Indonesia. *The International Journal of Human Resource Management, 21*(5), 754–780.

Pellegrini, E. K., & Scandura, T. A. (2008). Paternalistic leadership: A review and agenda for future research. *Journal of Management, 34*(3), 566–593.

Peterson, S. J., Galvin, B. M., & Lange, D. (2012). CEO servant leadership: Exploring executive characteristics and firm performance. *Personnel Psychology, 65*(3), 565–596.

Pollard, C. W. (1997). The leader who serves. *Strategy & Leadership, 25*(5), 49–51.

Quick, J. C. (1992). Crafting an organizational culture: Herb's hand at Southwest Airlines. *Organizational Dynamics, 21*(2), 45–57.

Schaubroeck, J., Lam, S. S. K., & Peng, A. C. (2011). Cognition-based and affect-based trust as mediators of leader behavior influences on team performance. *Journal of Applied Psychology, 96*(4), 863–871.

Schneider, S. K., & George, W. M. (2011). Servant leadership versus transformational leadership in voluntary service organizations. *Leadership & Organization Development Journal, 32*(1), 60–77.

Sendjaya, S., Sarros, J. C., & Santora, J. C. (2008). Defining and measuring servant leadership behaviour in organizations. *Journal of Management Studies, 45*(2), 402–424.

Senge, P. M. (1990). The leader's new work: Building learning organizations. *Sloan Management Review, 32*(1), 7–24.

Sergiovanni, T. J. (1992). *Moral leadership: Getting to the heart of school improvement.* San Francisco: Jossey-Bass.

Shahin, A. I., & Wright, P. L. (2004). Leadership in the context of culture: An Egyptian perspective. *Leadership & Organization Development Journal, 25*(6), 499–511.

Tepper, B. J. (2007). Abusive supervision in work organizations: Review, synthesis, and research agenda. *Journal of Management, 33*(3), 261–289.

Washington, R. R., Sutton, C. D., & Feild, H. S. (2006). Individual differences in servant leadership: The roles of values and personality. *Leadership & Organization Development Journal, 27*(8), 700–716.

West, G. R. B., & Bocarnea, M. C. (2008). *Servant leadership and organizational outcomes: Relationships in United States and Filipino higher educational settings.* Annual Roundtables of Contemporary Research & Practice, Regent University, Virginia Beach, VA.

Yoshida, D., Sendjaya, S., Hirst, G., & Cooper, B. (2014). Does servant leadership foster creativity and innovation? A multi-level mediation study of identification and prototypicality. *Journal of Business Research, 67*(7), 1395–1404.

Yukl, G. (1990). *Leadership in organizations.* Englewood Cliffs: Prentice-Hall.

Servant Leadership Research

One of the first questions I ask my students in my undergraduate leadership class is, "What first comes to your mind when you hear the word leadership?" As this occurs every semester, I think I have heard every possible answer students could give, reaching a saturation point. In one occasion following a typical interaction on that subject, a rather assertive student caught me off-guard not with his answer but with his reply, "What about you? Having done the run-of-the-mill on leadership, what now comes to your mind when you hear that word?" There was silence for a few seconds. I reflected a bit and came up with the following reply: "Leadership is ubiquitous and elusive!"

Why? Because leadership is almost an omnipresent theme that occurs in many different fields of human study – anthropology, social psychology, human relations, sociology, education, political science, theology, or business. As such, if a sociologist, a politician, and a theologian sit together to discuss leadership, chances are they will end up with big disagreements with each other.

A comprehensive listing of leadership research includes more than 8,000 leadership studies ranging from the great man theory in the early 1900s to contingency theory in the 1970s, and excellence theory in 1980s (Bass 1990). Yet the multidisciplinary nature of leadership contributed to the failure of leadership research to produce a systematic, coherent, and integrated understanding of leadership (Bass 1990). So much for the hype in leadership research that leadership researchers like Barnard (1948, p. 80) lamented in frustration over six decades ago and concluded that "leadership is the subject of an extraordinary amount of dogmatically stated nonsense." It is therefore importance to examine more closely the theoretical underpinning of and empirical support for servant leadership.

© Springer International Publishing Switzerland 2015
S. Sendjaya, *Personal and Organizational Excellence through Servant Leadership*,
Management for Professionals, DOI 10.1007/978-3-319-16196-9_2

2.1   Origin of Servant Leadership

Dubbed as the father of the servant leadership movement, Robert K. Greenleaf (1977) constructed the notion of servant leadership following his long career at AT&T. The process however was unconventional in that he did not based his theorizing on key corporate leaders or high profile individuals, but on his personal reading of Herman Hesse's (1956) story about a spiritual pilgrimage, *The Journey to the East*:

> In this story we see a band of men on a mythical journey . . . The central figure of the story is Leo, who accompanies the party as the servant who does their menial chores, but who also sustains them with his spirit and his song. He is a person of extraordinary presence. All goes well until Leo disappears. Then the group falls into disarray and the journey is abandoned. They cannot make it without the servant Leo. The narrator, one of the party, after some years of wandering, finds Leo and is taken into the Order that had sponsored the journey. There he discovers that Leo, whom he had known first as servant, was in fact the titular head of the Order, its guiding spirit, a great and noble leader. (Greenleaf 1977, p. 7)

It was in Hesse's character of Leo that Greenleaf (1977) saw an interesting juxtaposition between servanthood and leadership. Specifically, Leo's leadership is evident through his capability to facilitate a group of pilgrims to achieve a shared objective, and his servanthood through his meeting their needs. The moral of the story lies in the fact that leadership and servanthood are not mutually exclusive.

The idea that leaders must serve their constituents has been around much longer. To show this point, Nair (1994, p. 59) points to ancient monarchs who for over a thousand years had at least professed the importance of service to leadership:

> Ancient monarchs acknowledged that they were in the service of their country and their people – even if their actions were not consistent with this. Modern coronation ceremonies and inaugurations of heads of state all involve the acknowledgement of service to God, country, and the people. Politicians define their role in terms of public service.

Attributing the notion of servant leadership entirely to Greenleaf (1977) however would constitute an intellectual sloppiness. Granted it was Greenleaf (1977) who first introduced and disseminated it to the education and business arena. But the principle of servant leadership has been taught and embodied by Jesus Christ and his disciples over 2,000 years ago, much earlier than the works of Greenleaf or Hesse. While the exact terminology was non-existent anywhere in the Bible, a cursory reading of both the Old Testament and New Testament shows that the idea of leaders serving their people is deeply embedded in numerous passages that speak about leadership.

Surveying the biblical accounts of servant leadership is simply beyond the scope of this book, it is nevertheless instructive to look at two particular instances in the Bible where Jesus Christ taught and demonstrated servant leadership as recorded in the Gospel of Mark Chapter 10 and Gospel of John Chapter 13, respectively.

Jesus' life and ministry occurred primarily in Galilee, a large rural province in the northwestern part of Palestine ruled under the Roman Empire. The ruling regime in his days was the Roman political government who recruited local Jewish religious leader who were recognized and respected by the native populations but were loyal to Rome in exchange for positions and prestige. They worked well together to maintain stability in the region, and had been known to suppress any movement that might endanger the delicate balance of power. In the beginning of Jesus' ministry of teaching, feeding the hungry, healing the sick, and casting out evil spirits, he was careful not to undermine their respective authorities, dismissing the crowd and withdrawing from them when his growing followers asked him to be their king. However towards the end of his short three-and-a-half-year ministry, he started to reveal his identity to the public as the expected Messiah the Jewish prophets of old had foretold. The Jewish leaders were quickly disturbed to see an increasing number of people following him as he made his journey from Galilee to Jerusalem to make a final sacrifice for the people he served.

During that journey that took a few days by foot, Jesus foretold his imminent death to his inner circle of twelve disciples at the hands of corrupt religious leaders three times. However they seemed to fall on deaf ears. The talk of Jesus' death was repeatedly brushed aside as the disciples were preoccupied with a different subject in their minds. They were anxious about the succession plan in what they thought would be the ultimate empire of the Messianic kingdom in the world. Who among them would be a worthy successor of this supremely authoritative and much sought-after man?

In a self-aggrandizing mode, they were intensely arguing against each other to claim superiority. The constant bickering and jockeying for power must have destroyed the harmony among the disciples. From that point onwards they would have been suspicious of each other's motives. Against this background, Jesus taught his disciples the principle of servant leadership:

> You know that those who are considered rulers of the Gentiles lord it over them, and their great ones exercise authority over them. But it shall not be so among you. But whoever would be great among you must be your servant, and whoever would be first among you must be slave of all. For even the Son of Man came not to be served but to serve... (Mark 10:42–45, ESV)

In this example, Jesus used the term 'servant' as a synonym for greatness. Contrary to the popular opinion of the day, Jesus taught that a leader's greatness is measured by a radical commitment to serve fellow human beings.

Shortly following that incident, Jesus demonstrated in a most practical way what it means to serve others through the symbolic act foot-washing common to Palestinian Jews of his day. In the Gospel of John chapter 13 we had the account of the first-century foot-washing ritual. To appreciate its significance, a few cultural nuances need to be properly understood (Ford 1991). First, the ritual was regularly performed for practical rather than ceremonial reasons. As people wore sandals everyday and walked through dusty, muddy, and manure-filled streets, one cannot avoid having dirty and smelly feet. And they need to be washed. Needless to say, washing someone else's feet was regarded as one of the most demeaning tasks anyone could perform. Second, it was customary at the time that whenever someone invites people over for a meal, the host would provide a servant to wash the guests' feet before they came to the table. In poor families where no servant was employed, it was common for the lowest-ranking guest to wash the feet of the others (Ford 1991).

Neither Jesus nor his disciples had their feet washed when they entered a house to have a meal together. They sat at the table with dirty feet, as there was no household servant present and none of the disciples took the initiative to do it. Shortly after the evening meal was served, Jesus abruptly got up. The Bible recorded that he "laid aside his outer garments, and taking a towel, tied it around his waist. Then he poured water into a basin and began to wash the disciples' feet and to wipe them with the towel that was wrapped around him (John 13:4–5 ESV).

This socially unacceptable gesture must have come as a shock to his disciples, and at the same time served as an unambiguous example of servant leadership for us. Jesus concluded the lesson in memorable words: "If I then, your Lord and Teacher, have washed your feet, you also ought to wash one another's feet. For I have given you an example, that you also should do just as I have done to you (John 13:14–15 ESV).

It was not so much the actual foot-washing that he stipulated. Rather it was the readiness of leaders to set aside their ego to be able to serve others wholeheartedly. As such, the unusual twist of Jesus' leadership through the foot-washing example redefined the meaning and function of leadership power from 'power over' to 'power to'; that is, the strength to choose to serve others.

More broadly, many passages in the Bible either explicitly or implicitly teach about servant leadership. While there are only six occurrences of the term 'leader' in the King James Bible because individuals called to be spiritual leaders are designated as 'servants'. When Moses in the Old Testament was called to lead the Israelites out of Egypt and into Canaan, he was not referred to as "Moses, my leader", but "Moses, my servant."

Unfortunately a persistent neglect of the etymology of the word 'servant' in the New Testament today continues to cause a gross misunderstanding of the idea of servant leadership. The negative connotations associated with 'leaders as servant' may not persist if one considers the amount of scholarly work in the field of biblical exegesis around the word 'servant'. *Merriam-Webster Online* dictionary might give a clue to the richness of this biblical word picture when it defines 'servant' as 'one that serves others' or 'one that performs duties about the person or home of a master or personal employer.'

As the most ancient yet richest text that explicitly presents the concept of 'servant' in depth, the New Testament uses seven Greeks words interchangeably which unfortunately are simplified into one word in the English bible, i.e., 'servant'. These Greek words are *diakonos, doulos, pais, sundoulos, oiketes, therapon*, and *huperetes* (Vine 1985). Altogether these words occur over 300 times in the New Testament (Getz 1984). Each of these words has its own association with the cultural settings of the biblical times. A close scrutiny of these words using bible dictionaries and Greek lexicon indicates that the concept of 'servant' is pregnant with meaning.

For example, the word *diakonos* literally means 'someone who waits at the table', referring to the person who renders service during a meal (Bennett 1998) as depicted in Jesus' parable in the Gospel of Luke (17:8). Implicit in the usage of the word are lessons for disciples to wait at the table and serve others instead of sitting at the head-table and seeking to be served. The English word 'deacon' is derived from *diakonos*, which is commonly used to describe a church leader. *Diakonos* is also significant because it is used to describe Jesus' lessons about servant leadership. Embedded within the use of the word *diakonos* is the emphasis on humility and selfless service. Hence, in Jesus' terms, leadership is not about power and personal aggrandizement, but about offering oneself in service to others.

Doulos is the most frequently used word for 'servant' in the New Testament both in literal and figurative sense (Getz 1984). Literally speaking, the word simply denotes the natural condition of those who live as slaves to their masters (Vine 1985). However, contrary to the common understanding, the use of *doulos* in the Bible refers to the notion of subjection without the idea of bondage. The same emphasis is also found in the figurative use of the word *doulos* in the New Testament (Vine 1985). The word *doulos* was frequently used metaphorically to describe positive spiritual, moral and ethical conditions (i.e. in bondage of God) as well as negative connotations (e.g. in bondage of sin or corruption). On the whole, while the word *doulos* was often taken in its strongest sense to mean a slave who gives himself up to another's will in disregard of his own interests, it signifies a voluntary act of subordination performed in the context of Christian love for God and others. This voluntary subordination is manifested in the willingness to assume the lowliest of positions and endure hardship and suffering on behalf of other people.

Pais signifies an attendant, particularly the king's attendant (Vine 1985).

Sundoulos means fellow servant, which corresponds to the notion of an associate or colleague who is subject to the same authority (Thayer 1996).

Oiketes, which is the root of the English word 'economy', refers to a household servant who lives in the same house as the householder (Locyker 1986).

Therapon denotes an attendant or servant of God and spoken with dignity of Moses who faithfully carried out the duties assigned to him by God (Thayer 1996).

Huperetes literally means an under-rower or subordinate rower, which signifies "those who row in the lower tier of a trireme (an ancient Greek three-tiered warship), and then came to mean those who do anything under another, and hence simply 'underlings'" (Robertson and Plummer 1914, p. 74). In the contemporary sense, it could well be translated as 'subordinate'. In short, these words denote a servant who submits to the authority of and is accountable to his superior.

Taken together, the seven Greek words for servant suggest a willingness and readiness to be subservient before others in obedient gratitude, so that others' needs and interests are served. None of these words insinuate a lack of self-respect or low self-image. While some words may indicate that the subordination is imposed on someone because of his or her lowly status, the humble position is voluntarily assumed and an act of service is wholeheartedly performed for the sake of others.

2.2   Servant Leadership and Other Theories

Given the elusive nature of leadership and ubiquity of leadership studies, the extent
to which servant leadership, relative to other leadership approaches, affects key
organizational outcomes is critical. This is particularly relevant in light of the fact
that there is little empirical evidence that suggests leadership style X provides higher
levels of outcome Z than leadership style Y (Peterson et al. 2012). To that end,
servant leadership is often contrasted to charismatic, transformational, authentic,
and spiritual leadership. The following sections briefly examine the theoretical and
empirical distinctions among these leadership approaches.

2.2.1   Charismatic and Transformational Leadership

Among the early research on charisma, probably the single most important work
was written by the sociologist Max Weber (1947) whose primary interest was in the
dynamic forces of authority in society. Weber argues that charismatic leadership is
essentially a perception by followers that a leader possesses a divinely inspired gift
which makes him or her larger than life. Weber's most frequently cited definition
of the Greek word charisma is "a quality of an individual personality by virtue of
which he is set apart from ordinary men and treated as endowed with supernatural,
superhuman, or at least specifically exceptional qualities" (Weber 1947, p. 48). This
form of influence is based not on a traditional view that authority is inherited,
or on a rational-legal view that authority is derived from appointment to certain
positions, but rather on followers' perceptions and beliefs that leaders are gifted with
extraordinary and exemplary qualities which set them apart from ordinary people.
In addition to that, Weber maintains that charismatic leaders are grass-roots leaders
emerging from marginalized society during times of great social crisis. Often times,
they arise as the result of a revolution against traditional or legal-rational authority
systems.

Weber's conceptualization of charismatic authority systems has attracted a
number of comments from historians, political scientists, and sociologists. Since
the publication of Weber' seminal book The Theory of Social and Economic
Organization where the notion of charisma is conceived, research into charismatic
leadership has focused around the locus of charismatic leadership. The focal
question is whether charisma is the result of the leader's divine supernatural gift,
the strong cohesion between charismatic leaders and followers, social context the
leader faces, or merely an attribution-based phenomenon (Weber 1947; House 1977;
Bass 1985; Bennis and Nanus 1985; Tichy and Devanna 1986; Conger and Kanungo
1987).

Among those who are considered as charismatic leaders are mostly those in the
political domain: Alexander the Great, Adolf Hitler, John F. Kennedy, and Winston
Churchill; social-religious figures: Jesus Christ, Mahatma Gandhi, Reverend Jim
Jones, Mother Teresa, the Ayatollah Khomeini, Martin Luther King, Jr., and

Nelson Mandela; those in the military domain: Norman Schwartzkopf, Napoleon Bonaparte, Joseph Stalin, Saddam Hussein, and Colin Powell; and those in business: Lee Iacocca, Jack Welch, and Mary Kay Ash (Kets de Vries 1989; Yukl 1990). A common thread among these political, social, religious, military and business leaders is their alleged possession of personal magnetism and heroic qualities which have strong effects on followers, societies, countries, or organizations.

Despite increasing empirical evidence on the validity of charismatic leadership in positive organizational and social changes reported by its proponents, some critical questions have been raised. Major objections to the research on charismatic leadership concern the rather dark and often subtle aspects of charisma, especially toward those whom the leader's influence is being exerted upon (Bass 1985; Howell 1988; Kets de Vries 1995; Graham 1991; Gronn 1995). Kets De Vries (1993, 1995) contends that there are charismatic leaders who are psychologically "unhealthy." From a clinical paradigm, he argued that these leaders are capable of making their internal illusions of power and control into social and physical reality, which makes them particularly dangerous people. Another important comment that concerns the negative side of charisma maintains that there are two types of charismatic leaders, socialized and personalized (Howell 1988). Socialized charismatic leaders are oriented toward the development of their followers, whereas personalized charismatic leaders create within their followers feelings of obedience, dependency, and submission to the goals and desires of leaders.

Negative charismatic leaders are self-centered, whereas positive charismatic leaders are oriented toward others. Conger (1991) contended that three particular leadership skills might contribute to disastrous outcomes for both organizations and followers, namely leaders' strategic visions, their communication and impression-management skills, and their general management skills. The distinction between positive and negative charismatic leaders is critical to take into consideration (Howell 1988; Yukl 1989; Conger 1991) since:

> History is full of accounts of charismatic leaders who cause untold death, destruction, and misery in the process of building an empire, leading a revolution, or founding a new religion. Many entrepreneurs who founded prosperous companies were tyrants and egomaniacs. Negative charismatics are likely to have a narcissistic personality and a personalized power orientation. They emphasize devotion of followers to themselves rather than to ideological goals, which are used only as a means to manipulate followers. (Yukl 1990, p. 231)

Bass (1985) expanded further the concept of charismatic leadership into what he calls 'transformational leadership' based on Burns' (1978) notion of 'transforming leadership'. Although there are substantial similarities between charismatic and transformational leadership, and are therefore often regarded as equivalent, the latter is generally defined more specifically than the former. There is a disagreement, however, as to whether the two terms can be used interchangeably or distinguished (Yukl 1990). Yukl (1999) concludes that it is best to differentiate the two types of leadership regardless their overlapping processes. Nevertheless, it is important to underline that, as Bass argues, charisma is the most important ingredient of transformational leadership although not the only one (Bass 1985).

Apart from charisma, there are two other ingredients necessary to turn the transformation process into reality, namely intellectual stimulation and individualized consideration (Bass and Avolio 1994). Proponents of transformational leadership argue that transformational leaders will cause followers to perform beyond expected levels of performance as a consequence of the leader's influence. Followers are willing to go the extra mile because of their commitment to the leader, their intrinsic work motivation, or the sense of purpose and mission that drives them to excel beyond the standard limit. Since charisma is a key construct underlying transformational leadership behavior, attaining charisma in the eyes of one's employees is central to succeeding as a transformational leader. As listed by House (1977), this charisma often times results in, among other things, the followers' unquestioning acceptance of the leader, strong identification with the leader, trust in the correctness of the leader's belief, and willing obedience.

Graham (1991) gave credit to the addition of the two developmental behaviors in transformational leadership. These behaviors acknowledge the followers' inherent capabilities of constructive creativity and give room for followers to question the leader's espoused views. On the other hand, she critically pointed out its lack of concern about the moral development of the followers. In fact, she noticed two flaws in Bass' (1985) model of transformational leadership, namely its manipulative leadership style and the incompatibility of the model with the original model on which it was based on, i.e., Burns'(1978) transforming leadership.

Bass (1985) argued that transformational leaders seek to empower and elevate followers rather than keep followers weak and dependent. However the effects of that increased motivation and commitment will not necessarily benefit followers, as 'there is nothing in the transformational leadership model that says leaders should serve followers for the good of followers' (Graham 1991, p. 110). On the other hand, servant leadership requires that leaders lead followers for the followers' own ultimate good.

Stone et al. (2004) suggested that while both servant leadership and transformational leadership are people-oriented leadership approaches which value individualized consideration and appreciation of followers, the concerns that transformational leaders show are merely a means to achieving a larger purpose, namely the organizational objectives. On the other hand, the focus of servant leaders is primarily on the followers (i.e. their needs and development) rather than the organization. In fact, servant leadership is more likely than transformational leadership to put an emphasis on employee emotional well-being (Smith et al. 2004).

Unlike transformational leadership whose primary concern is 'performance beyond expectations, the *sine qua non* of servant leadership is followers' holistic moral and ethical development. In fact, from its earliest conceptualization, servant leadership has been considered a leadership approach that elevates leaders and followers both morally and ethically (Greenleaf 1977).

In summary, servant leaders have a greater likelihood than transformational leaders to set the following priorities in their leadership focus: followers first, organizations second, their own last. Rather than inspiring followers to achieve organizational goals, they empower, coach, train, and develop followers into what they

Table 2.1 Graham's comparison of four models of charismatic leadership (Graham 1991)

	Weberian charismatic	Personal celebrity charisma	Transformational leadership	Servant leadership
Source of charisma	Divine gift	Personality; Social distance	Leader training & skills	Humility; spirituality insight
Situational context	Socio-economic distress of followers	Ennui; low self esteem of followers	Unilateral (hierarchical power)	Relational (mutual power)
Nature of charismatic gift	Visionary solution of Distress	Daring; dramatic; flair; forcefulness; vision	Vision for organizational adept at HRM	Vision and practice of a way of life focused
Response of followers	Recognition of genuinely Devine gift	Adulation of the identification with leader	Heightened motivation; extra effort	Emulation of leader's service orientation
Consequences of charisma	Followers' material well-being improved	Co-dependent relationship with leader perpetuated	Leader and/or organizational goals met; personal development of followers	Autonomy and moral development of followers; enhancement of common good
Applicability to work organizations	No	Yes	Yes	Yes
Representative authors and concepts	Tucker; Weber	Conger & Kanungo; Howell's 'personalized charisma'; Schiffer	Bass & assoc; Bradford & Cohen; Howell's 'socialized charisma'	Burns' "transforming leadership"; Greenleaf

are capable of becoming. The rationale behind this deliberate focus on followers is well summarized by Stone et al. (2004, p. 355) who asserted that "organizational goals will be achieved on a long-term basis only by first facilitating the growth, development, and general well-being of the individuals who comprise the organization". The focus therefore is on 'people-building' rather than 'people-using'.

Graham (1991) regarded servant leadership as one of the charismatic leadership models with some characteristics that distinguish it from other previous three models (see Table 2.1). The model is represented by two main authors' concepts: Burn's (1978) transforming leadership and Greenleaf's (1977) servant leadership. Graham also argues that the servant leadership concept exceeds Bass' (1985) transformational leadership at least in two ways; in its recognition of the leaders' social responsibilities to serve those people who are marginalized by a system and its dedication to followers' needs and interests, as opposed to those of their own or their organization (Graham 1991).

2.2.2   Authentic Leadership

Authentic leadership refers to a leadership approach that nurtures and fosters a sense of self-awareness, an internalized moral perspective, balanced processing of information, and relational transparency (Walumbwa et al. 2008, p. 94). As such, authentic leaders are those who operate out of a deep clarity of their own values and conviction. This propensity to be self-aware and self-regulating is well aligned with the authenticity dimension of servant leadership (Avolio and Gardner 2005). Both authentic and servant leaders use positive modeling to develop others. However, the authenticity of servant leaders stems out of a spiritual and moral source of motivation tempered with an altruistic desire to serve others. These spirituality, morality, and altruistic dimensions are largely absent from the authentic leadership framework. Servant leaders are authentic not the sake of being authentic but because they know that they are driven by a sense of higher calling to make morally positive difference in the lives of others.

A recent empirical study found that leaders who possess superior moral reasoning does not necessarily exhibit moral action despite how authentic they perceive themselves to be or other people think they are (Sendjaya et al. 2014). In fact, the same study found that one could score high on both authenticity and Machiavellianism, and that the two are not mutually exclusive. This counterintuitive finding can be explained by the need for authentic leaders to maintain a sense of self-concordance, that is they act in alignment with their beliefs regardless of the cost or the consequences, or else they stop being morally authentic. However, their self-concordance is entirely based on their internal choices rather than externally imposed standards (Hannah et al. 2011). Since authenticity is bound by one's subjective view of ethics and morality, it is plausible for unethical leaders to claim themselves to be authentic as long as their behaviors align with their beliefs. In a stark contrast, servant leaders rely on objective moral values external to themselves to derive their judgment about what is right and wrong. Fully aware of their susceptibility to moral errors as human beings, they would not base their decisions and actions solely on their preconceived notion of morality. In summary, in the realm of ethics, being morally accountable to some objective standards takes priority over being congruous to one's subjective morality. Further discussion on the morality of servant leaders is provided in Chap. 6.

2.2.3   Spiritual Leadership

While the notion of spiritual leadership is abound in the popular press, empirical studies on the subject were scarce. A notable exception is Fry (2003) whose spiritual leadership model has a few points of convergence with the servant leadership framework outlined in this book. Specifically both seek to cultivate in the workplace a sense of meaning, purpose, and interconnectedness in the workplace. Spiritual leaders engage individuals in meaningful and intrinsically motivating work, through vision, altruistic love, and hope/faith (Fry 2003). These three variables are also embedded in the construct of servant leadership but there is more to servant leadership than what is captured by the spiritual leadership theory.

Further in Fry's (2003) model, the notion of calling and membership are the outcomes of followers' spiritual survival. They are however inherent in servant leadership as evident in the sense of inner calling servant leaders have which fuels their service, and their aspiration to foster leader–follower relationships characterized by shared values and mutual trust.

The key difference between the two theories is as follows. Spirituality is only one of the many dimensions of servant leadership (i.e., *Transcendental Spirituality*). Specifically, spiritual insights are motivational basis for servant leaders to engage others in authentic and profound ways that transform them to be what they are capable of becoming. There other leadership dimensions within the servant leadership framework such as servanthood and morality which are absent in the spiritual leadership model.

2.3   Positive Effects of Servant Leadership

Critics argue that given its focus on followers' need and development, servant leadership will not positively contribute to the bottom line, at least not directly. Recent studies however have reported evidences in support of the positive impacts of servant leadership on various soft and hard measures of corporate performance.

In fact, in addition to the conceptual differences in its focus and scope relative to other leadership approaches, these evidences unequivocally suggest that servant leadership is a better predictor than transformational leadership in relation to a few key outcome variables. More specifically, as mentioned in Chap. 1, in comparison to transformational leadership, servant leadership explains additional variance on a number of key outcomes including team performance, employee satisfaction, organizational commitment, and intention to stay (Schaubroeck et al. 2011; Schneider and George 2011; Liden et al. 2008; Peterson et al. 2012).

In addition to the above studies, the studies that my colleagues and I have conducted help corroborate the evidence for positive effects of servant leadership on key organizational outcomes such as creativity and innovation, trust, organizational citizenship behavior, job satisfaction, and employee engagement. These studies are particularly of interest as they employed the multidimensional measure of Servant Leadership Behavior Scale (SLBS). The following section provides a brief summary of the studies, demonstrating that servant leaders do make a difference in real-world settings.

2.3.1   Creativity and Innovation

In a multi-level study employing a two-nation East Asian sample of 154 teams, my colleagues and I examine the mediating social psychological processes by which servant leaders stimulate individual creativity and team innovation (Yoshida et al.

2014). The findings suggest that under a strong climate of support for innovation, servant leadership stimulates followers' relational identification which in turn, foster employee creativity.

Since servant leaders voluntarily subordinate their aspirations for the greater good of the team and organization, they exemplify many of the team characteristics. On the basis of relational identification theory, we argue that team members' affect-based trust in the servant leader encourage them to define themselves in terms of their relationship with the leader. As the servant leader is seen as a prototypical leader, team members heighten their intrinsic motivation to perform creatively. Broadly speaking servant leaders' primary objectives are not specifically linked to creativity, particularly when it does not directly benefit followers. However, the strong association of followers' identity with the leader-follower relationship creates a powerful and personal motivation for followers to embark in creative endeavors. Team members who derive their identity from a close-knit leader-follower relationship are also more willing to experiment with new ideas because there is a strong sense of psychological safety embedded in such relationship.

Practically speaking, the study findings highlight the need for servant leaders to intentionally build psychological connections with team members to foster employee creativity and team innovation. Generating followers' trust, identification, and perceptions that the leaders represent the team's beliefs, norms and attitudes becomes more critical when creativity and innovation is a priority organizational goal. Secondly, servant leaders need to build a team climate which encourages creative endeavors and innovative ideas at the individual and team level.

2.3.2 Trust in Leaders

In another study which examines the impact of servant leadership on followers' trust in their leaders using data from 555 employees of two educational institutions, Sendjaya and Pekerti (2010) found that followers who perceived high servant leadership behavior in their leaders had significantly higher trust in them compared with those who perceived low servant leadership behavior in their leaders. Employees may decide to trust the organization on the basis of the trust they have in the leader. When such generalization of trust does not occur, employees are likely to trust only their leader but not the organization.

The results contribute to extant leadership literature by demonstrating that servant leadership is a significant predictor of trust. Three out of six dimensions of servant leadership (Covenantal relationship, Responsible morality and Transforming influence) were found to correlate positively and significantly to trust. Organizations should therefore encourage their leaders to exhibit trust-building servant leadership behaviors, such as articulation of a shared vision, role modeling, demonstration of concern and respect for followers, and integrity-infused decisions and actions.

2.3.3 Organizational Citizenship Behavior

Another study utilized 123 leader-follower dyads in eight high-performing companies in Indonesia to examine the relationship between servant leadership and organizational citizenship behavior (OCB) (e.g., does not take extra break, obeys company rules) (Butarbutar et al. 2012). The study found that psychological ethical climate served as an important mediator in the relationship between servant leadership and individual-directed citizenship behavior (OCBI) as well as organization-directed citizenship behavior (OCBO) Specifically, the link between servant leadership to OCBI is stronger than servant leadership to OCBO.

This finding implies that servant leaders may stimulate followers to demonstrate assistance in regard to other co-workers' needs (OCBI-type behavior) more than the followers' intention to read and keep up with organization announcements or memos (OCBO-type behavior). More practically, managers need to be aware of what they pay attention to, where their passions and priorities are, what they handsomely reward or severely punish, how they spontaneously react to crisis situations, all of which will help foster an ethical culture in the organizations which will guide the employees' perceptions and actions accordingly.

2.3.4 Job Satisfaction

In their study, Eva and Sendjaya (2013a) examine extent to which organizational structure (formalization and centralization) and leaders' decision making process (involvement and dominance) moderate the relationship between servant leadership and job satisfaction in small to medium enterprises. On the basis of two independent studies, vignette experiment (n = 1,569) and cross-sectional survey (n = 336), the impact of servant leadership on job satisfaction is contrasted with narcissistic leadership in the vignette experiment, and with transformational leadership controlled for in the survey.

The underlying assumption of the study is that leaders do not operate in a vacuum but interact with the boundary constraints found in the organizational setting. The study found that leader's decision making process and organisational structure acts as boundary conditions for servant leadership to impact employee job satisfaction. Specifically, when servant leaders are highly involved in the decision making process and operate under a formalised structure, their effects on job satisfaction are augmented. On the contrary, when they are dominant and operate under a centralised structure, servant leaders have less impact on the followers' job satisfaction.

2.3.5 Employee Work Engagement

Finally, another study by Robin and Sendjaya (2012) on the relationship between positive leadership behaviors, psychological capital, employee work engagement, as well as destructive workplace deviant behavior in Australian firms. Data were collected from Australian organizations across different industries (N = 441). The study found that psychological capital is the mechanism through which servant leadership influences employee engagement and workplace deviant behaviors. It is therefore important for servant leaders to cultivate employees' psychological capital through positive feedback, psychological arousal, and vicarious modeling, and mastery of experience as these means are key in enhancing employee engagement and minimizing workplace deviant behavior.

2.4   Development of the Servant Leadership Behavior Scale

This section briefly outlines the development and validation of the Servant Leadership Behavior Scale (SLBS). The psychometric measure went through a number of sequential stages, namely scale design (domain identification and item development), scale development (content validation and pretest), and scale validation (construct validation).

2.4.1   Scale Design

The main purpose of this first stage was to generate a pool of items for a multidimensional rating scale of servant leadership (i.e., the SLBS). The current study employed a combination of deductive and inductive approaches to item development with both the literature review and interviews carefully conducted to generate items. Although development of items is the most important element of establishing sound measures, an overwhelming majority of leadership measures demonstrate a lack of content validity. As such, the generation of items was meticulously done to ensure that the SLBS sufficiently captures the specific domain of interest and excludes irrelevant items.

A comprehensive literature review of more than 350 leadership journal articles and books on was conducted to identify themes and dimensions pertinent to servant leadership. In-depth interviews with 15 executives at Australian for-profit and not-for-profit organizations were subsequently conducted to generate further insights into servant leadership. Content analyses of the interview data were subsequently conducted, and an initial coding template was developed as a theoretical framework used to categorize interview data (see 'Interview Method' in the Appendix for further details). Only servant leadership values that were supported by the literature review were included in the subsequent stages. Interrater reliability was established by an independent rater and a satisfactory agreement was reached.

Twenty-two values were identified as a result and were grouped into the six resulting domains, each defined accordingly consistent with the literature. On the basis of these findings from qualitative data, 101 items for the SLBS were generated with a clear theoretical underpinning.

2.4.2   Scale Development

The initial 101 items of the SLBS were subjected to content expert validation in order to establish its content validity. Content experts made up of leadership researchers were asked to select and sort out items that operationalize its nominated domain and those which are theoretically incoherent. They were also asked to evaluate the comprehensiveness of the measure and clarity of item construction and wording to ensure that there were no ambiguous and poorly expressed items. A quasi-quantitative approach called the Content Validity Ratio was utilized to facilitate the rejection or retention of specific items (see Sendjaya et al. 2008 for details). This process facilitated the decisions to reject or retain items, accounting for the deletion of 28 items. There were 73 remaining items with a high level of agreement (87 %) among content experts, suggesting that these items were parsimonious, theoretically essential, and conceptually meaningful.

The factor structure of the 73 items was then examined in a pretest involving post-graduate students with work experience (n = 277). The main purposes of the pretest were to examine the factor structure of the scale and establish the unidimensionality of the scale through specification, assessment of fit, and respecification of the one-factor congeneric measurement models. The internal consistency reliabilities of and the correlations among the six factors were well within the accepted range. Exploratory and confirmatory factor analyses using structural equation modeling were performed to examine the one-factor congeneric measurement models of the SLBS. The modeling established the unidimensionality of the SLBS with a total of 35 items retained in the process.

2.4.3   Scale Validation

The 35-item six-factor model of the SLBS was further tested using an independent survey of management and non-management staff at four Australian organizations (n = 192). All of the six models yielded Cronbach's coefficient alphas beyond the recommended level which demonstrated the reliability of the scale. The correlations among the six factors were consistent with those from the pretest data, which suggest that servant leadership is a holistic construct (e.g., an individual who scored high on *Responsible Morality* would be likely to score high on *Authentic Self* and vice versa). In order to establish discriminant validity of the six factors, analyses of competing models were performed to examine whether the six factors were empirically distinguishable from each other. Analysis of fit indices revealed that the six-factor model was a good-fitting model to both data sets. To provide further evidence of construct validity, the convergent and discriminant validity of the SLBS were established in relation to two other measures, namely the Character Assessment Rating Scale or CARS (convergent validity) and the Machiavellianism scale or MACH-IV (discriminant validity). The problem of common method variance was addressed using the latent variable approach to marker variables. These results suggested that the six-factor model was a robust model.

In summary, the use of multiple qualitative and quantitative methods comprising interview respondents from various organizations, external and independent expert panels, and survey respondents from the student sample and organizational sample satisfied the criteria of triangulated data. Through successive stages of scale development, the study identified a list of operational indicators (i.e., the 35-item 6-factor SLBS) that satisfied important validity criteria, namely content validity, internal consistency reliability, and unidimensionality (for details, see Sendjaya et al. 2008), as well as construct, discriminant, and convergent validity (for details, see Sendjaya and Cooper 2011). Other studies using the SLBS have continued to demonstrate its predictive validity (Pekerti and Sendjaya 2010; Sendjaya and Pekerti 2010; Yoshida et al. 2014) and practical usefulness (Eva and Sendjaya 2013a, b).

2.5   Objections to Servant Leadership

Over the past 10 years or so, I have received comments from journal editors and reviewers as well as research study and executive workshop participants on perceived theoretical problems with servant leadership. While these inputs clarified my own understanding, some of them were derived logically from a flawed interpretation of the concept. An earlier version of these objections has appeared elsewhere (Sendjaya 2011), but I have expanded the discussion to include other key objections.

2.5.1   "Servant Leaders? I Don't Want to Be Slaves!"

The above sentiment reflects the most pervasive misunderstanding of servant leadership that stops many from even considering the idea. The phrase 'servant leadership' conjures up in their minds negative images associated with the dark ages such as slavery and bondage. The unpleasant and embarrassing memory of slavery that dwells in many parts of the English-speaking world make the language of slavery offensive to them. In my experience I have been asked in a number of occasions by corporate clients who are interested to undertake the servant leadership training program to alter the word 'servant' into something that is more politically correct. Invariably I nodded in agreement with them and said, "Okay, let's not use *servant leadership*. Instead let's roll with *slave leadership*!"

This widespread misconception is unfortunate because if a close scrutiny of the Bible, one of the oldest literatures that includes the concept and practice of slavery, reveals that there is a huge difference between the nature of slavery in the first century Greco-Roman world and sixteenth century New World. In his fine work explicating the nature of slavery in the Bible by comparing Jewish, Greek,

Roman, and ancient slavery in the first century BC, Harris (1999, p. 44) reached the following conclusion:

> In the first century, slaves were not distinguishable from free persons by race, by speech or by clothing; they were sometimes more highly educated than their owners and held responsible professional positions; some persons sold themselves into slavery for economic or social advantage; they could reasonably hope to be emancipated after ten to twenty years of service or by thirties at the latest; they were not denied the right of public assembly and were not socially segregated (at least in the cities); they could accumulate savings to buy their freedom; they natural inferiority was not assumed.

It is estimated that during that the end of the first century BC in Italy there were two million slaves out of a total population of six million. They worked in various occupations from farm laborers to city clerks, from cooks to shop managers, from cleaners to salaried executives of the state or a business (Harris 1999). Since the institution of slavery as part of a way of life, however, no doubt there were malpractices and abuses that occurred. But broadly speaking it was in a stark contrast to the coercion-based and morally reprehensible sixteenth century institution of slavery which led to its abolition in the second half of the eighteen century.

The second misconception of servant leadership stems from the failure to understand that the difference between the literal and metaphorical use of slavery in the New Testament books of the Bible. Again Harris (1999) is instructive when he argues that the Christian teaching primary focuses on the metaphorical or figurative language of slavery rather than literal or physical. Regarding the latter, following a comprehensive survey of extant literature, Harris (1999) concluded that Christianity did not endorse slavery as an absolute possession or inhuman use of one human being by another, yet at the same time the movement was not focused on social reform to abolish slavery as a social institution but on the transformation of character and conduct. While the biblical teaching of equality and freedom slowly led to the eventual destruction of physical slavery, the burden of the New Testament teaching rests on the metaphorical slavery to depict one's relation to God or Christ. Harris (1999, p. 86) summarizes it well as follows:

> So, then, in true Christian liberty, freedom *from* is immediately succeeded by freedom *for*. We are set free from slavery to sin precisely in order to be free to choose slavery to Christ, a slavery of perfect freedom. . . Such a transfer of allegiance, such an exchange of masters, saves us from failing prey to the danger of using liberty as an opportunity or pretext for evil and the danger of becoming liberty's slave.

The Apostle Paul modeled this when he wrote to the Corinthian church, "Though I am free and belong to no one, I have made myself a slave to everyone, to win as many as possible" (1 Corinthians 9:19, NIV Bible). Inspired partly by this verse, church father Martin Luther (1943, p. 5) penned these words which I think should be a building block for a healthy understanding of servant leadership (as this is written in the 1940s, do not let its gender-specific language deters its meaning): "A

Christian man is a perfectly free lord of all, subject to none. A Christian man is a perfectly dutiful servant of all, subject to all." Applied to servant leadership, it essentially means that in relation to their liberating God, servant leaders are subject to nobody with respect to liberty, subject to everyone with respect to service.

In summary, the association between servant leadership and the sixteenth century slavery stems from an ignorance of the nature of slavery. It will be a remiss to jettison altogether the construct of servant leadership on the basis of an unfounded fear that the practice of servant leadership will see the proliferation of modern day slavery. Indeed it will be a classic case of throwing the baby with the bathwater. The following comment of a director of not-for-profit organization in my interview sample best captures the sentiment:

> I think you can do exactly the same thing with sex. I mean sex is fantastic, it's the perfect expression of love. But you can commercialize it, you can twist it, and you can make it a very ugly aspect. Just look at child prostitution for example. Similarly, work is an excellent concept through which one could express his or her talents to the full, but you can twist it too. Think about workaholism. The principle of servanthood is a wonderful concept, but you can turn it into slavery. It's taking something that is pure and good, and twisting it. And I think you can do that with anything.

2.5.2 "Are Servant Leaders Doormats?"

Given the altruistic motive with which servant leaders serve others, would they not be treated as doormats and their altruism misused or abused? The concept of accountability embedded in servant leadership sheds light on the above concern. Block (1993) argued that servant leaders view themselves as stewards who hold themselves accountable for the wellbeing and growth of the people they serve. It is however relatively easy these days to cite accountability merely as a compliance exercise. Marshall (1991, p. 72) distinguished between accepting accountability as a matter of reactive obligation and proactive or voluntary choice, and maintained that servant-first leaders choose the latter as "they are accustomed to being answerable to their performance." As a natural expression of their true servanthood, servant leaders seek to be accountable not only to the people they serve but also to others (e.g, board of directors, other stakeholders of an organization, the leader's personal core values and moral integrity). Hence, the accountability of servant leaders towards their followers is not absolute in that servant leaders will be subservient to followers' demands. On the other hand, servant leaders' accountability to their followers is tempered by other accountability structures and relationships they consciously put themselves in. The interplay between accountability and service in servant leadership relationships is perhaps best captured by the phrase "I am your servant, but you are not my master" as outlined in the following remark in the interview:

> Call it 'I am your servant, but you are not my master'. . . If you think servant leadership is just giving the people what they want . . . you are actually missing the generous nature of

true servant leadership. Your relative accountability is to the people you work with and who work for you. So you do have a relative accountability then, but it's not absolute.

2.5.3 "Servant Leadership Is for Religious People"

Is it true that servant leadership has such a heavy religious overtone that it leaves out people who do not associate themselves with certain religions or religious beliefs. A cursory review of extant literature reveals that servant leadership is typically linked to some religious teaching. The majority of servant leadership publications have both explicit and implicit links to the Judeo-Christian theology although many emerging publications also link servant leadership to other religious teachings. Robert Greenleaf, dubbed as the grandfather of servant leadership, was a Quaker but drew heavily on Hesse's Journey to the East steeped in ancient Eastern religious mysticism as well as Carl Jung's atheistic notion of self-consciousness. Greenleaf's conceptualization of servant leadership therefore reflects a syncretic view which merges two discrete theological presuppositions and traditions. It is important to note, however, that servant leadership has also found support from non-religious beliefs (see for example, Fry 2003; Hicks 2002).

Kurth (2003), for example, argued that the concept of service is taught by all major religions (e.g. Islam, Christianity, Judaism, Hinduism, Buddhism) and non-religious philosophies (e.g. moral philosophy, Siddha yoga, Taoism). To illustrate, one of Immanuel Kant's (1964, pp. 32–33) famous categorical imperatives, "Act in such a way that you always treat humanity, whether in your own person or in the person of any other, never simply as a means, but always at the same time as an end" strongly captures the most important tenet of servant leadership.

In summary, practicing servant leadership does not require one to subscribe to a particular religion or religious belief. For those of some religious persuasion, servant leadership emerges from an internal conviction that the servant leader is a servant of a higher being or power, and in obedient gratitude to that higher being or power, serves other people. Tyson Foods, one of world's largest processors and marketers of food products, have long flourished in a faith-friendly workplace culture (Rossi 2014). John Tyson, the company's Chairperson, created a workplace chaplaincy program in 2000 run by team members from a variety of religious faith backgrounds to serve the needs of the employees and their family members regardless of their religious affiliation or beliefs, include those who claim no affiliation at all. Its CEO Donnie Smith openly declared that his faith influences how he thinks think and what he does as he leads the multinational company by serving his employees.

For those with spiritual orientation but no religious attachment, the motivation to practice servant leadership comes from not a higher being, but a set of core values or ideals or causes that partly or wholly define their lives and give them meaning and significance.

2.5.4 "Servant Leadership Is an Oxymoron"

One reason for the scarcity of research on servant leadership is that the oxymoronic notion of 'servant as leader' may deter potential research in the area. It may be difficult to think and act both as leader and servant at the same time – a leader who serves and a servant who leads. Paradox has been characterized as "the simultaneous presence of contradictory, even mutually exclusive elements (Cameron and Quinn 1988, p. 2). While the notion of paradox has received increasing attention from management and organizational scholars (see, for example Kets De Vries 1995), studies on paradox are severely hindered by the limitations associated with traditional research methods. Rooted in and relying on logic and rationality, traditional approaches are unfit for examining paradoxical tensions which are seemingly absurd and irrational (Lewis 2000). More contemporary approaches, however, consider paradox as a means to substantially enhance management theories by contributing insights into complex and ambiguous organizational interrelationships (Cameron and Quinn 1988; Poole and Van de Ven 1989).

Clegg et al. (2002) noted that sustaining juxtaposing opposites rather than resolving them often leads to syntheses that enhance the practice and understanding of management. Lewis (2000), for example, cites a study on the paradoxical nature of group dynamics which concludes that the strength of a group or team can best be achieved by managing the tension between collective affiliation and self-expression. Based on the finding that the extent to which the individuality of each team member is expressed is a key to team success, researchers unveil an important lever in maximizing team performance. A similar pattern emerges through careful examination of opposing perspectives such as stable structures and the dynamic processes of authority and empowerment (Westenholz 1993). Implied in the above examples of simultaneous occurrences of two seemingly conflicting phenomena is the need of a 'both/and' thinking approach, as opposed to 'either/or', to manage paradox (Lewis 2000).

Similarly, the seemingly absurd and irrational coexistence of servanthood and leadership contains a profound understanding of leadership. Plett (1997, p. 2) used the analogy of marriage to explain the paradox of servant leadership: "Servant and leader, like a married couple, stand in close proximity to each other and influence each other. Each is incomplete without the other; neither loses its independent identity." Sharing a similar view, Greenleaf (1977) drew his notion of servant leadership from Herman Hesse's (1956) Journey to the East paradoxical portrayal of the servant Leo whose servanthood comes through in his leadership. This metaphorical story of a pilgrimage inspired Greenleaf (1977, p. 8) to conceptualize the paradox of servant leadership embodied in Leo's character: "Leadership was bestowed upon a man who was by nature a servant. It was something given, or assumed, that could be taken away. His servant nature was the real man, not bestowed, not assumed, and not taken away. He was servant first."

2.5.5 "Which One Comes First: Influence or Service?"

One the biggest conundrums in the servant leadership field is its underlying influence process. If the hallmark of servant leaders is their deliberate choice to serve others and desire to serve first, does that signify followership rather than leadership? If the primary focus of servant leaders is to serve, how does a servant exert influence over others with leadership authority expected of a leader? Does the *servant-first* step mean that someone began as servants who serve some leader and/or team members and rise to leadership in a unique way?

Servant leadership stems from a conviction of the heart to transform other people with moral courage and spiritual insights into what they are capable of becoming. In servant leadership relationships, the leaders acts as stewards, that is they consider their followers as people who have been entrusted to them to be elevated to their better selves and to be what they are capable of becoming. Followers tend to respond well to servant leaders because they have proven themselves trustworthy as servants. And since leadership is more 'caught' than 'taught', followers themselves will be transformed into servant leaders. The transformational effects in followers is achieved through what is often perceived as a counterintuitive way, that is servant leaders willingly sacrificing their needs and wants in order to serve others, instead of serving their own selves by sacrificing other people. As an other-orientated rather than leader-centered leadership approach, the effectiveness of the servant leadership approach is therefore measured by the holistic development of both the leaders and followers.

The conviction to serve others does not preclude the responsibility on the part of the servant leader to exert influence. While servant leaders seek to transform others to be more servant-like, there is a higher purpose that both the leaders and servants mutually seek to accomplish. Servant leaders try to get others to achieve that higher purpose by way of service. Service therefore is a means to try to role model ideal behaviors and values that are aligned with this higher purpose. To put it differently, servant leaders seek to influence first, and choose the path of servanthood to accomplish that task.

The paradox therefore is not between leadership and service but lies on the ordering of service and influence. Does service or influence come first? I think servant leaders have an influence agenda that they try to apply on the followers. In this sense, servant leaders are visionary individuals who have a clear idea of the kind of leaders that they expect their followers to become. This vision will in the final analysis benefits the followers, and may or may not benefit the leaders. If servant leaders first serve other individuals, would their acts of service be driven mainly by the individual level needs and aspirations and marked by the absence of a greater purpose or unifying principle? In my view, servant leaders on the one hand accept others with unconditional acceptance and unqualified acceptance and on the other hand transform others to become the very people they are capable of becoming. Just like parents who love their children unconditionally but are committed to help them learn and grow to fully realize their full potentials, servant leaders accept followers as they are but seek to transform them to be better servant leaders. It is therefore accurate to conclude that there is a higher purpose that servant leaders pursue namely to turn followers into servant leaders, and that they employ service to try to role-model these behaviors.

This is clearly shown in the example of Jesus Christ as outlined in the Bible. Jesus did have a higher purpose, that is to influence others to live their lives in loving obedience to his Father. Jesus' life was a reflection of that higher purpose, and his sole preoccupation was to try to get others to do the same (i.e., influence) by engaging in self-sacrifice service to them. In this light, Jesus was a leader seeking to influence first, and chose the path of servant leader to accomplish that task. Hence, servant leaders can choose to serve others in an attempt to model ideal behaviors, but the intent remains to influence someone to see the vision of the greater good, or at least that leader's interpretation of the greater good. It is therefore appropriate to view servant leadership as a dyadic theory where there is a unique one-on-one relationship between leader and follower.

References

Avolio, B. J., & Gardner, W. L. (2005). Authentic leadership development: Getting to the root of positive forms of leadership. *The Leadership Quarterly, 16*(3), 315–338.

Barnard, C. I. (1948). *Organizations and management.* Cambridge, MA: Harvard University Press.

Bass, B. M. (1985). *Leadership and performance beyond expectations.* New York: Free Press.

Bass, B. M. (1990). *Bass and Stogdill's handbook of leadership* (3rd ed.). New York: The Free Press.

Bass, B. M., & Avolio, B. J. (1994). *Improving organizational effectiveness through transformational leadership.* Thousand Oaks: Sage.

Bennett, D. W. (1998). *Leadership images from the New Testament.* Carlisle: OM Publishing.

Bennis, W. G., & Nanus, B. (1985). *Leaders: The strategies for taking charge.* New York: Harper & Row.

Block, P. (1993). *Stewardship: Choosing service over self-interest.* San Francisco: Berrett Koehler.

Burns, J. M. (1978). *Leadership.* New York: Harper & Row.

Butarbutar, I. D., Sendjaya, S., & Härtel, C. E. J. (2012). *Servant leadership and citizenship behavior: The moderating effects of cultural orientations.* Paper presented in at the 2012 Academy of Management Annual Meeting, Boston, MA.

Cameron, K. S., & Quinn, R. E. (1988). Organizational paradox and transformation. In R. E. Quinn & K. S. Cameron (Eds.), *Paradox and transformation: Toward a theory of change in organization and management* (pp. 12–18). Cambridge, MA: Ballinger.

Clegg, S. R., da Cunha, J. V., & e Cunha, M. P. (2002). Management paradoxes: A relational view. *Human Relations, 55*(5), 483–503.

Conger, J. A. (1991). The dark side of leadership. *Organizational Dynamics, 19*(1), 44–55.

Conger, J. A., & Kanungo, R. (1987). Toward a behavioral theory of charismatic leadership in organizational settings. *Academy of Management Review, 12,* 637–647.

Eva, N., & Sendjaya, S. (2013a). *Servant leadership and job satisfaction: Moderating roles of decision making process and structure.* Paper presented at the 2013 Academy of Management Meeting, Lake Buena Vista, FL.

Eva, N., & Sendjaya, S. (2013b). Creating future leaders: An examination of youth leadership development in Australia. *Education + Training, 55*(6), 584–598.

Ford, L. (1991). *Transforming leadership: Jesus' way of creating vision, shaping values and empowering change.* Downers Grove: InterVarsity Press.

Fry, L. W. (2003). Toward a theory of spiritual leadership. *Leadership Quarterly, 14*, 693–727.

Getz, G. A. (1984). *Serving one another*. Wheaton: Victor.

Graham, J. (1991). Servant-leadership in organizations: Inspirational and moral. *Leadership Quarterly, 2*(2), 105–119.

Greenleaf, R. K. (1977). *Servant leadership*. Mahwah: Paulist Press.

Gronn, P. (1995). Greatness re-visited: The current obsession with transformational leadership. *Leading & Managing, 1*(1), 14–27.

Hannah, S. T., Avolio, B. J., & Walumbwa, F. O. (2011). Relationships between authentic leadership, moral courage, and ethical and pro-social behaviors. *Business Ethics Quarterly, 21*(4), 555–578.

Harris, M. J. (1999). *Slave of Christ*. Downers Grove: InterVarsity Press.

Hesse, H. (1956). *Journey to the East*. London: P. Owen.

Hicks, D. A. (2002). Spiritual and religious diversity in the workplace: Implications for leadership. *Leadership Quarterly, 13*(2), 379–396.

House, R. J. (1977). A 1976 theory of charismatic leadership. In J. G. Hunt & L. L. Larson (Eds.), *Leadership: The cutting edge* (pp. 189–207). Carbondale: Southern Illinois University Press.

Howell, J. M. (1988). Two faces of charisma: Socialized and personalized leadership in organizations. In J. A. Conger & R. N. Kanungo (Eds.), *Charismatic leadership: The elusive factor in organizational effectiveness* (pp. 213–236). San Francisco: Jossey-Bass.

Kant, I. (1964). *Groundwork of the metaphysics of morals* (H.J. Paton, Trans.). New York: Harper.

Kets De Vries, M. F. R. (1989). *Prisoners of leadership*. New York: Wiley.

Kets De Vries, M. F. R. (1993). *Leaders, fools, and impostors: Essays on the psychology of leadership*. San Francisco: Jossey-Bass.

Kets De Vries, M. F. R. (1995). *Life and death in the executive fast lane: Essays on irrational organizations and their leaders*. San Francisco: Jossey-Bass.

Kurth, K. (2003). Spiritually renewing ourselves at work: Finding meaning through serving'. In R. A. Giacalone & C. L. Jurkiewicz (Eds.), *Handbook of workplace spirituality and organizational performance*. New York: M.E. Sharp.

Lewis, M. W. (2000). Exploring paradox: Toward a more comprehensive guide. *Academy of Management Review, 25*(4), 760–776.

Liden, R. C., Wayne, S. J., Zhao, H., & Henderson, D. (2008). Servant leadership: Development of a multidimensional measure and multi-level assessment. *The Leadership Quarterly, 19*(2), 161–177.

Locyker, H. (1986). *Nelson's illustrated Bible dictionary*. Nashville: Thomas Nelson.

Luther, M. (1943). *A treatise on Christian liberty. Vol 2 of the works of Martin Luther* (p. 312). Philadelphia: Muhlenberg Press.

Marshall, T. (1991). *Understanding leadership: Fresh perspectives on the essentials of New Testament leadership*. Chichester: Sovereign World.

Nair, K. (1994). *A higher standard of leadership: Lessons from the life of Gandhi*. San Francisco: Berrett-Koehler.

Pekerti, A., & Sendjaya, S. (2010). Exploring servant leadership across cultures: Comparative study in Australia and Indonesia. *International Journal of Human Resource Management, 21*(5), 754–780.

Peterson, S. J., Galvin, B. M., & Lange, D. (2012). CEO servant leadership: Exploring executive characteristics and firm performance. *Personnel Psychology, 65*(3), 565–596.

Plett, S. (1997). Defining servant leadership. Steinbach Bible College Newsletter, p. 1–6.

Poole, M. S., & Van de Ven, A. H. (1989). Using paradox to build management and organization theories. *Academy of Management Review, 14*(4), 562–578.

Robertson, A., & Plummer, A. (1914). *A critical and exegetical commentary on the first epistle of St Paul to the Corinthians*. Edinburgh: T. and T. Clark.

Robin, M., & Sendjaya, S. (2012). *Leadership behaviors, employee engagement, and workplace behaviors: A multi-level perspective*. Paper presented at the 3rd Global Servant Leadership Round Table, Melbourne, Australia, 21–22 June.

Rossi, H.L. (2014, November 11). 7 CEOs with notably devout religious beliefs. *Fortune*.

Schaubroeck, J., Lam, S. S. K., & Peng, A. C. (2011). Cognition-based and affect-based trust as mediators of leader behavior influences on team performance. *Journal of Applied Psychology, 96*(4), 863–871.

Schneider, S. K., & George, W. M. (2011). Servant leadership versus transformational leadership in voluntary service organizations. *Leadership & Organization Development Journal, 32*(1), 60–77.

Sendjaya, S. (2011). Multidimensionality of servant leadership. In D. Van Dierendonck & K. Patterson (Eds.), *Servant-leadership: Recent developments in theory and research* (pp. 39–51). London: Palgrave.

Sendjaya, S., & Cooper, B. (2011). Servant leadership behavior scale: A hierarchical model and test of construct validity. *European Journal of Work and Organizational Psychology, 20*(3), 416–436.

Sendjaya, S., & Pekerti, A. A. (2010). Servant leadership as antecedent of trust organizations. *Leadership and Organization Development Journal, 31*(7), 643–663.

Sendjaya, S., Sarros, J. C., & Santora, J. C. (2008). Defining and measuring servant leadership behaviour in organizations. *Journal of Management Studies, 45*(2), 402–424.

Sendjaya, S., Pekerti, A., Härtel, C., Hirst, G., & Butarbutar, I. (2014). Are authentic leaders always moral? The role of Machiavellianism in the relationship between authentic leadership and morality. *Journal of Business Ethics.* doi:10.1007/s10551-014-2351-0.

Smith, B. N., Montagno, R. V., & Kuzmenko, T. N. (2004). Transformational and servant leadership: Content and contextual comparisons. *Journal of Leadership & Organizational Studies, 10*(4), 80–91.

Stone, A. G., Russell, R., & Patterson, K. (2004). Transformational versus servant leadership: A difference in leader focus. *Leadership & Organization Development Journal, 25*(4), 349–261.

Thayer, J. (1996). *Thayer's Greek-English Lexicon of the New Testament* (Reissueth ed.). Peabody: Hendrickson Publishers.

Tichy, N. M., & Devanna, M. A. (1986). *The transformational leader.* New York: Wiley.

Vine, W. E. (1985). *Vine's expository dictionary of biblical words.* Nashville: Thomas Nelson.

Walumbwa, F. O., Avolio, B. J., Gardner, W. L., Wernsing, T. S., & Peterson, S. J. (2008). Authentic leadership: Development and validation of a theory-based measure. *Journal of Management, 34*, 89–126.

Weber, M. (Ed.). (1947). *The theory of social and economic organization.* New York: Free Press.

Westenholz, A. (1993). Paradoxical thinking and change in the frames of reference. *Organization Studies, 14*(1), 37–50.

Yoshida, D., Sendjaya, S., Hirst, G., & Cooper, B. (2014). Servant leadership, creativity, and innovation. *Journal of Business Research, 67*(7), 1395–1404.

Yukl, G. (1989). Managerial leadership: A review of theory and research. *Journal of Management, 15*(2), 251–289.

Yukl, G. (1990). *Leadership in organizations.* Englewood Cliffs: Prentice-Hall.

Yukl, G. (1999). An evaluation of conceptual weaknesses in transformational and charismatic leadership theories. *Leadership Quarterly, 10*(2), 285–305.

Voluntary Subordination

3

> *Enlightened leadership is service, not selfishness. The leader grows more and lasts longer by placing the well-being of all above the well-being of self alone. Paradox: By being selfless, the leader enhances self.*
>
> (Lao Tzu, as cited in Heider 1986 p. 13)

Selfless service has been singled out throughout the ages as the leadership non-negotiable prerequisite, as shown in the above quote by a sixth century BC Chinese philosopher Lao Tzu. Fast forward 2,000 years, and we will find modern-day leadership authors echoing the same sentiment: "True leadership is achieved not be reducing men to one's service but in giving one's selfless service to them (Sanders 1994, p. 15).

Since selfless service represents the hallmark of servant leadership, it is instructive to correctly capture the nuance of the phrase 'voluntary subordination'. The phrase 'voluntary subordination' is not a common phrase in the vernacular of leadership. In fact it would not be the first thing that comes to mind when people hear the slippery L word. I adapted this unusual phrase from Foster (1989) who described leadership as a revolutionary act of will to voluntary abandon one's self to others. According to Foster (1989), the willingness to abandon self in service to others is exemplified most visibly in the leadership of Jesus of Nazarene in the Bible. This upside-down leadership can also be observed in other leaders such as Mohandas Gandhi, Martin Luther King, Jr., Jack Lowe of TDIndustries, Arne Sorenson of Marriott and countless others who never made it to history or business texts. Let me unpack why the phrase fittingly describes the defining dimension of servant leadership.

The operative word 'voluntary' suggests that the leaders subordinate themselves because they want to, not because they have to. The decision to serve others stem from a willing heart, suggesting a conscious and deliberate choice. No doubt the notion of subordinating ourselves to others is subversive in our contemporary

© Springer International Publishing Switzerland 2015

S. Sendjaya, *Personal and Organizational Excellence through Servant Leadership*,
Management for Professionals, DOI 10.1007/978-3-319-16196-9_3

context for obvious reasons. Every cell in our bodies screams against the idea of subordinating ourselves to others. Indeed we have come a long way to be able to embrace that people are created equal, and should enjoy the freedom to pursue our natural inclination to get ahead of others. Everyone in the modern world knows this by heart. Those in leadership positions do understand that pursuit so well they take it one step further and pursue it more aggressively at all costs.

But let us examine our ambivalence towards power. By definition leaders have the ambition to be ahead of people, propelling them to accumulate more experience, knowledge, expertise, authority, influence, and other sources of power. A classic theorizing of sources of power by French and Raven (1959) maintains that social power originates in five distinct sources which can contradict as well as reinforce each other – expert power, referent power, reward power, coercive power, and legitimate power. The sense of exhilaration that comes with possession of power often subtly triggers an unhealthy dose of narcissism or excessive self-love (Kets de Vries 1993). Such erosion of power occurs in a gradual manner however that many leaders fail to recognize its emergence and domination upon themselves. As the leaders gain the pinnacle of control, the power they are initially willing to share become something they anxiously hoard and reserve for themselves. It will be remiss for leaders to ignore the fact that "power is a powerful narcotic – animating, life-sustaining, addictive. The people who have it generally have worked hard to obtain it and are not overkeen to let it go" (Kets De Vries 1993, p. 38).

In its naked form, power often manifests as power over other people. The history is riddled with cases of leaders preoccupied with power, guarding it, wielding it, and maintaining it at all costs. Such leaders first manage their power, then before long their power manages them. It is worth noting that it is not always power that corrupts. Clinical psychology research repeatedly confirms that the roots of abusive power are often found in men and women who were once victimized by power. While Lord Acton's oft quoted maxim – "Power tends to corrupt and absolute power corrupts absolutely" still haunts many corporate leaders today, the exact opposite of that maxim Edgar Friedenberg once wrote provides a more sober understanding of the reason why power corrupts – "All weakness tends to corrupt and impotence corrupts absolutely." It is powerlessness, whether perceived or real, that often propels people to attain and wield power in destructive ways. When victims become perpetrators, the damage caused is escalated to a much greater proportion.

Our ambivalence towards power is not unwarranted. We squirm those who abuse power and undermine those who possess none. Granted leaders have to exercise power to be able to lead others yet the issue at stake is how to do it wisely and responsibly as there are enormous, subtle ethical challenges in the exercise of power (Hollander 1995). Armed with power at their disposal, leaders should be responsible and held accountable for the choice they make – whether they choose destructive power to dominate and manipulate or creative power used to serve and inspire.

The latter choice allows leaders to exercise servant leadership. Servant leaders are fully aware of the ambivalent nature of power, and consciously treat power as 'power for others' rather than 'power over others'. They perceive power as an empowering factor for them to choose to serve. Think of a man who finds it impossible to forgive his friend who had done him wrong. Gandhi once said, "The weak can never forgive. Forgiveness is the attribute of the strong. " Only those who are strong enough to refuse to be imprisoned by feelings of anger, bitterness, and self-pity can have the freedom to choose forgiveness. In a similar vein, both powerless-turned-power-hungry and powerfully corrupt leaders never have the privilege to choose to serve. Serving is the attribute of the strong. The weak struggle to serve because they are under the tyranny of their own inordinate desire to be served and prioritized.

The strength of servant leaders to serve others voluntarily lies in understanding the difference between having power and having a need for power. The former refers to something that has already been in one's possession; the latter, a desire for a higher degree of that something. While servant leaders possess power, they have a low need for power (Graham 1991). They do not perceive power as something to be pursued and amassed but rather as something that naturally flows from who they are (e.g., character strength) and what they do (e.g., behavioral integrity). Since they are not power-hungry, they are likely to have a low tendency to mistreat power, which enables them to have a genuine motive to serve others. This is portrayed in the selfless life of Jesus of Nazareth who declined the request of Jewish people of his day to make him a king. He becomes a perfect example of a genuine servant leader who "though he was in the form of God, did not count equality with God a thing to be grasped, but emptied himself by taking the form of a servant . . . " (The Bible, ESV, Philippians 2:5–7).

Nelson Mandela is another clear example of voluntary subordination in practice. Serving his South African fellow citizens through the Truth Commission, he led the nation to deal with hatred, violence, and crimes against humanity during the Apartheid Era. His aspiration to serve and willingness to walk the road of sacrifice that led him to the position of leadership stemmed not from his lust for power, but his love for his people. In later years as a powerful leader, he transcended revenge and embraced his enemies and tormentors in reconciling love. His humility and his sense of forgiveness kept him from being deceived by dark side of power.

In the corporate arena, one can turn to William Pollard, former chairman of The ServiceMaster company, to gain inspiration for voluntary subordination. His company has been recognized by Fortune magazine as the number one service company among the Fortune 500 firms for consecutive years. Exemplifying a servant's hearts in his leadership, he contends that the real leader is not the "person with the most distinguished title, the highest pay, or the longest tenure, . . . but the role model, the risk taker, . . . the servant; not the person who promotes himself or herself, but the promoter of others" (Pollard 1997, pp. 49–50).

The aforementioned individuals demonstrate that it is their voluntary choice to harness power as an immeasurable good in service of others. Rather than using power to serve their needs, servant leaders give up personal rights so they can effectively serve others. Nair (1994, p. 59) captures this sentiment as he reconciles two seemingly contradictory issues power and service in leadership:

Many of us have come to believe that leadership is the attainment of power. But as long as power dominates our thinking about leadership, we cannot move toward a higher standard of leadership. We must place service at the core; for even though power will always be associated with leadership, it has only legitimate use; service.

Two values are associated with the dimension of *Voluntary Subordination*, namely being a servant and acts of service.

3.1 Being a Servant

Servant leaders view themselves as the servant first, as distinguished from leaders first "who later serves out of promptings of conscience or in conformity with normative expectations" (Greenleaf 1977, p. 14). Viewed this way, servant leaders are natural servants who lead rather than natural leaders who serve. Servant leadership therefore emerges from the aspect of the leader's 'being', as opposed to 'doing'. It is instructive to note the sequence of the phrase 'servant leader'. Leadership is often considered the operative word, and servant is the qualifier. But according to the aforementioned theorizing, a more fitting phrase then is not servant leaders but *leading servants*. It refers to people who will serve the organizational mission and vision in alignment with its core values and lead others to do the same.

However more essential than focusing on the semantics is ensuring that servant leadership is about *being* rather than *doing* (Jaworski 1997). As such it is a manifestation of the leader's orientation of character. To put it differently, servant leaders demonstrate a resolute conviction and strong character by taking on not only the role of a servant, but also the nature of the servant. It is above all an attitude of the heart, which finds expression in the leader's ingrained pattern of living. This emphasis on being was on Jesus' mind when he described himself to his followers in the following way: "I am among you as one who serves" (NIV Bible, Gospel of Luke 22:27). This identification corresponds with Greenleaf's (1977, p. 13) assertion that "the servant leader is a servant first". Accordingly, the primary intention of servant leadership is servanthood, not leadership (De Pree 1989; Farling et al. 1999; Wright 2000). Lorne Sanny, the president of a student ministry organization, once asked by a businessman how he could tell if one is truly a servant leader. He responded by pointing to one's initial and candid response when he is treated as a servant. If the person feels offended and launches a defensive mechanism to protect his hurting ego, chances are he is not a true servant.

Being a servant constitutes the self-concept of the servant leader. The notion of self-concept has been associated with self-image, self-esteem, self-perception, and self-awareness. As such at the most basic level, the leaders' self-concept involves the extent to which they are aware of their thoughts, beliefs and values. Like other individuals, leaders behave in ways consistent with their self-concepts (Sosik and Dworakivsky 1998). Therefore, servant leaders' primary intent to serve may emanate from their self-concept as altruistic individuals.

This attribute of *being a servant* is illustrated in the following comments taken from the interviews I conducted with executives working in various not-for-profit and for-profit organizations in Australia (details of the interview methodology are provided in the Appendix).

> When you're a servant leader, you look at the servant role as being your real responsibility. Your role is to lead, but the real responsibility is to actually make sure that you're serving . . . You need to be constantly reminded that you're the servant of the group.
>
> Servant leadership is not something that can be turned on or turned off. I think it's the way of being. I think it's the way of relating. I think if it's just a doing thing, then you tend to think of something you turn off and on in certain contexts. But if it's something that is part of your heart and your being, then that's the way you operate in terms of your family, your workplace, etc.

The comments above suggest that servant leadership is not merely the service that one performs (doing), but represents something deeper that reflects who the person is (being). The manifest content captured in those paragraphs such as *the servant of the group*, *the way of being*, and *the way you operate* alludes to the idea that servant leadership is more about inward reality than outward appearance. This attitude of the heart which resonates within servant leaders is evident, however, in their acts of practical and concrete services, putting other peoples' needs and interests above those of their own.

3.2 Acts of Service

The second sub-dimension of *Voluntary Subordination* is acts of service. It is unfortunate that leaders have often been portrayed in the academic and popular press as isolated heroes controlling and commanding others from within their ivory towers (Gronn 1995; Yukl 1989). In the organizational context, the word 'leader' has been mostly ascribed to people who hold management positions and are capable of giving orders to other members of the organization (Senge 1990). The common, principal motive for such larger-than-life Herculean leaders is to lead followers to achieve certain organizational objectives. While this is no doubt part and parcel of leadership, often the preoccupation with the organizational bottom lines led to a conscious neglect of followers.

The above orientation stands in sharp contrast to servant leaders whose main motive is to serve others to be what they are capable of becoming (Greenleaf 1977). The motivational element of servant leadership (i.e. to serve first) portrays a fundamental presupposition which distinguishes it from other leadership approaches. This presupposition forms the mental model of the servant leader, that is the "I serve" as opposed to the "I lead" mentality. To put it differently, the servant leader operates on the assumption that "I am the leader, therefore I serve" rather than "I am the leader, therefore I lead." The following case in point outlined by former Herman Miller CEO, Max De Pree (1992, pp. 218–219), helps illustrate the difference:

> I arrived at the local tennis club just after high school students had vacated the locker room. Like chickens, they had not bothered to pick up after themselves. Without thinking too much

about it, I gathered up all their towels and put them in the hamper. A friend of mine quietly watched me do this and then asked me a question that I've pondered many times over the years. "Do you pick up towels because you're the president of the company. Or are you the president because you pick up the towels?"

Two premises can be derived from the above modest incident: I serve because I am the leader ("I pick up towels because I am the president") and I am the leader because I serve ("I am the president because I pick up the towels"). While both premises imply a linear relationship between the act of service and the position of leader, they stand squarely opposite each other in terms of cause and effect.

The first premise 'I serve because I am the leader' signifies the act of altruism. Both Jesus' and Greenleaf's delineation of servant leadership put the emphasis on the acts of service, as opposed to the act of leading, of the leader. It is through that act of serving that the leaders lead other people to be what they are capable of becoming. The second premise 'I am the leader because I serve' begins with the deep-seated desire that one wants to lead, or the ambition to be prominent among others. The desire to be ahead of others may compromise the career endeavors or personal ambitions of leaders. For example, when Lee Iacocca decided to reduce his annual salary to one dollar to transform Chrysler Corporation, that action was undertaken to "convince employees of the need for sacrifice and extra effort" (Bass 1985, p. 15). However, Choi and Mai-Dalton (1998) questioned the authenticity of such action, commenting that it could merely be nothing but a tactic to impress followers and manipulate their responses to reciprocate.

Several authors have argued that the source of a servant leader's motivational base lies in either their principles, values and beliefs (Farling et al. 1999) or their humility and spiritual insights (Graham 1991). These intrinsic motivating factors enable servant leaders to take on the nature and the role of a servant. In fact, they enable servant leaders to engage themselves in self-sacrificial behaviors (Choi and Mai-Dalton 1998).

Often the servant attitude is most clearly seen in the trivial things that leaders do spontaneously, rather than the grand actions that leaders carefully orchestrate. They cheerfully engage in small, sometimes menial, tasks which are often overlooked. This includes for example the leaders making a cup of coffee for someone, washing the dishes after office functions, or even letting someone go through the door as illustrated in the following comments:

> It's often in the little things that the servant attitude is revealed rather than in the big things. Small attitudes. Attitudes to people. Attitudes to status. The leader who never makes a coffee for anybody else, always have one made for him. Things that you just pick up by just being around people and notice them . . . If you're around the person for a while, you can figure out whether they've got a servant attitude or not.
>
> I'll give you an example. Every month we have a special afternoon tea where people who have birthdays during that month will sing happy birthday, and we have a birthday cake, eat and so on. Now, you get a situation where traditionally as soon as the afternoon tea is finished, everybody just goes back to their desks. And all their plates are left. What happens is that the women of the group from the social conditioning perspective just naturally come together and they take their dishes and clean the kitchen. I make a point of it every now and then [to] help clean up the dishes. It's not only a reminder of them, but also a reminder

to me that just because I'm their boss doesn't make me exempt from washing the dishes. There are little things I do like that constantly

For example, a whole range of our people will work on the basis that we'll always let somebody go through a door before they do. Usually, it's only let the lady go first. But this is letting the other person go first, whether they are old, young, female, doesn't matter, we'll always stand back and let somebody else go first. Sort of the unwritten law here that the more senior you are in the so called hierarchy, the more you wait for others to go. That is a conscious reminder that we're always thinking about putting other people first no matter what it is. I think little things like that add up and help reinforce the sorts of behaviors that we want

Implicit in the above comments is the willingness of servant leaders to engage in practical and, sometimes, menial tasks to meet the personal and professional needs of others. The extent to which a servant leader is enthusiastic in serving others is observable by others through the way they interact with and treat others.

Another tangible expression of a leader's act of service is the discipline of responding to any problem by listening first. Greenleaf (1977) maintained that servant leaders possess a natural tendency to engage with others by listening with intent to understand, as opposed to merely pretending to listen or selective listening. Genuine listening develops strength in other people and transforms the relationship between the leader and the led (Covey 1991). Kim and Mauborgne (1992, p. 124) in their observation of a Chinese parable posited that leaders need to learn the art of listening to both the spoken and unspoken words of others:

For only when a ruler has learned to listen closely to the people's hearts, hearing their feelings uncommunicated, pains unexpressed, and complaints not spoken of, can he hope to inspire confidence in his people, understand something is wrong, and meet the true needs of his citizens. The demise of states comes when leaders listen only to superficial words and do not penetrate deeply into the souls of the people to hear their true opinions, feelings, and desires.

3.3 Self-Serving vs Servant Leaders

More in-depth examination of the construct of service however reveals that service can be misappropriated to serve one's end. As the ensuing discussion highlights, it is not too far-fetch to conclude that there are fake service and authentic service. How can we tell then if we are true servant leaders or chameleons who cleverly shape-shift into servant leaders for self-preservation and self-advancement purposes? The contrast between self-serving leaders and servant leaders is shown in the table below (Table 3.1).

Self-seeking leaders also serve others, but with a distorted motive, mission, method, and mode. They are willing to serve only when the service is grand enough to bring them significant gains in return. They tactfully serve the power holders in the organization because of the benefits or favors that they will receive in return. In fact, they can opt with their twisted sheer brilliance to serve the marginal people so that they can project a humble image to others. Further, for self-serving leaders, the willingness to serve is dictated by their moods. Whenever they experience physical

Table 3.1 Differences between self-serving leaders and servant leaders

	Self-serving leaders '*Sacrificing others, Serving self*'	Servant leaders '*Sacrificing self, Serving others,*'
Motive	Much efforts are spent on scheming strategies to render the service that attracts the most attention	Service flows naturally from the heart
Mission	Choose a service or whom to serve based on the potential return	Welcomes every genuine opportunity to serve within reason
Method	Serve after calculating the result, always requiring external reward	Serve because it is right, resting contented in hiddenness
Mode	Affected by moods, service is done only when convenient	Serve because there is a legitimate need as part of an ingrained lifestyle

fatigue, psychological numbness, relational problems, or even inadequate sleep, their readiness to serve evaporates accordingly. Throwing themselves into service in such conditions would result in resentful service, which can be easily detectable by the person on the receiving end. Hence, self-serving leaders serve others only when they feel they want to serve or when it is convenient for them to do so. This inconsistency of attitude contributes to their recurring insensitivity and indifference toward a legitimate need of service. Service is therefore nothing but a means to their end (Blanchard and Hodges 2003; Foster 1989; Marshall 1991; Wilkes 1998).

In contrast, servant leaders are more conscious of their responsibilities than their rights, readily taking up opportunities to serve others whenever there is a legitimate need regardless of the nature of the service, the person served, or the mood of the leader and without seeking acknowledgement or compensation. They engage with others in self-sacrificial behaviors, in the sense that they are willing to incur personal costs to serve others (Choi and Mai-Dalton 1998). The self-sacrificial nature of servant leaders provides a basis for their behaviors to be willingly emulated by their followers.

The greatness of servant leaders does not lie in the quantity of their direct reports or fans but in the type of people they serve. Their glory is not in their ability to spellbind their followers but their commitment to those who are ignored and marginalized. It was Charles Spurgeon (1877, p. 373) who first observed in the nineteenth century that serving without cost-and-benefit analysis is the acid test of one's character:

> I think you may judge a man's character by the persons whose affection he seeks. If you find a man seeking only the affection of those who are great, depend upon it he is ambitious and self-seeking; but when you observe that a man seeks the affection of those who can do nothing for him, but for whom he must do everything, you know that he is not seeking himself but that pure benevolence sways his heart

It is therefore fitting to conclude the chapter with the following thoughts:

> Servant leaders are not leaders who serve, rather they are servants who lead.
>   While those who serve may not necessarily lead, those who lead should serve.
>   Those who are unwilling to serve do not have the right to lead.

3.4   Actionable Commitments of Servant Leadership

The following seven commitments relate to the *Voluntary Subordination* dimension of servant leadership. They are part of the psychometrically valid measure of the Servant Leadership Behavior Scale (SLBS), hence can be used with confidence for personal reflection or group evaluation purposes. These commitments can be and have been used to inform selection, training, promotion, and performance evaluation of leaders in the organizations.

Commitment #1 – Consider others' needs and interests above your own
Do you tend to sacrifice others to serve yourself, or sacrifice yourself to serve others? Heed the advice of Lao Tzu in the opening quote above that the leader enhances self by being selfless. Build a habit to make yourself available at others' disposal. Ask someone, "If you can have me as your personal assistant for the next 10 min, how would you want to help you?" This sort of simple gesture can be quite contagious, making citizenship behaviors more prominent feature of the work culture.

Commitment #2 – Use power in service to others, not for your own ambition
If you have someone who reports to you, ask the person, "If you were me, what would be the number one thing you would do to help me become the best I can be?"

Commitment #3 – Be more conscious of your responsibilities than rights
Leadership positions come with perks and benefits, bells and whistles, often dwindling leaders into status-driven, self-focused creatures. Breaking free from the tyranny of self who always insists on rights gives a profound sense of freedom. Servant leaders are stewards, thus it is fitting to start the day with the question, "How can I best cultivate and grow those individuals entrusted to me today?"

Commitment #4 – Serves people without regard to their backgrounds (gender, race, age, personality, etc.)
Parents with at least two children will know that the only way for them to love their children the same is by loving them differently. Every child is different, and so is everyone at work. They each have a unique struggle, fear, and dream. Meet people where they are at their point of need, show respect for their individual feelings, and be a dealer of hope.

Commitment #5 – Demonstrates your care through sincere, practical deeds
Seek opportunities to engage in small tasks to assist your followers with their projects or concerns. It can be offering a cup of coffee or help fixing the paper jam in the photocopy machine. These ordinary, menial acts of kindness speak volume about your character, particularly if they directly relate to someone's specific situation.

Commitment #6 – Listens to others with intent to understand

Listening is more of a discipline than a skill since all it takes is for leaders to resist opening their mouth, and start opening their ears. Practice the discipline of listening by inviting people to share stories of their life. Be interested by probing the details using the 5W 1H questions (Why, where, when, who, what, and how). Paraphrase and show empathy to signal that you follow and understand.

Commitment #7 – Assists others without seeking acknowledgement or compensation

True altruistic acts are done in secret, the left hand should not know what the right hand is doing. Do something significant to others that cost you something (energy, time, money) and never tell anyone about it, and enjoy that sense of contentment that you have truly made a difference in others.

References

Bass, B. M. (1985). *Leadership and performance beyond expectations*. New York: Free Press.

Blanchard, K. H., & Hodges, P. (2003). *The servant leader: Transforming your heart, head, hands, & habits*. Nashville: J. Countryman.

Choi, Y., & Mai-Dalton, R. R. (1998). On the leadership function of self-sacrifice. *Leadership Quarterly, 9*(4), 475–501.

Covey, S. R. (1991). *Principle-centred leadership*. New York: Simon & Schuster.

De Pree, M. (1989). *Leadership is an art*. New York: Dell Publishing.

De Pree, M. (1992). *Leadership jazz*. New York: Dell Publishing.

Farling, M. L., Stone, A. G., & Winston, B. E. (1999). Servant leadership: Setting the stage for empirical research. *Journal of Leadership Studies, 6*(1/2), 49–72.

Foster, R. J. (1989). *Celebration of discipline*. London: Hodder & Stoughton.

French, J. R. P., Jr., & Raven, B. H. (1959). The bases of social power. In D. Cartwright (Ed.), *Studies in social power* (pp. 150–167). Ann Arbor: Institute for Social Research.

Graham, J. (1991). Servant-leadership in organizations: Inspirational and moral. *Leadership Quarterly, 2*(2), 105–119.

Greenleaf, R. K. (1977). *Servant leadership*. Mahwah: Paulist Press.

Gronn, P. (1995). Greatness re-visited: The current obsession with transformational leadership. *Leading & Managing, 1*(1), 14–27.

Heider, J. (1986). *The Tao of leadership: Leadership strategies for a new age*. New York: Bantam.

Hollander, E. P. (1995). Ethical challenges in the leader-follower relationship. *Business Ethics Quarterly, 5*(1), 55–65.

Jaworski, J. (1997). Destiny and the leader. In L. C. Spears (Ed.), *Insights on servant leadership: Service, stewardship, spirit, and servant leadership* (pp. 258–268). New York: Wiley.

Kets De Vries, M. F. R. (1993). *Leaders, fools, and impostors: Essays on the psychology of leadership*. San Francisco: Jossey-Bass.

Kim, W. C., & Mauborgne, R. A. (1992). Parables of leadership. *Harvard Business Review, 70*(4), 123–128.

Marshall, T. (1991). *Understanding leadership: Fresh perspectives on the essentials of New Testament leadership*. Chichester: Sovereign World.

Nair, K. (1994). *A higher standard of leadership: Lessons from the life of Gandhi*. San Francisco: Berrett-Koehler.

Pollard, C. W. (1997). The leader who serves. *Strategy & Leadership, 25*(5), 49–51.

Sanders, O. J. (1994). *Spiritual leadership*. Chicago: Moody Press.

Senge, P. M. (1990). The leader's new work: Building learning organizations. *Sloan Management Review, 32*(1), 7–24.

Sosik, J. J., & Dworakivsky, A. C. (1998). Self-concept based aspects on the charismatic leader: More than meets the eye. *Leadership Quarterly, 9*(4), 503–526.

Spurgeon, C. H. (1877). *The metropolitan tabernacle pulpit: Sermons.* New York: Passmore & Alabaster.

Wilkes, C. G. (1998). *Jesus on leadership: Discovering the secrets of servant leadership from the life of Christ.* Wheaton: Tyndale House.

Wright, W. C. (2000). *Relational leadership: A biblical model for influence and service.* Carlisle: Paternoster.

Yukl, G. (1989). Managerial leadership: A review of theory and research. *Journal of Management, 15*(2), 251–289.

Authentic Self

4

Either appear as you are or be as you appear.
(Mevlana, 1207–1273)

There are many ways to learn to be leaders. Googling leadership development for example will generate more than 85 million entries and may not be the best way to start. The more perceptive students of leadership will engulf themselves with thousands of scientific leadership studies to find some timeless wisdom on how to become effective leaders. Unfortunately these studies until very recently focused on discovering definitive patterns embodied in successful leaders in terms of their traits, characteristics, styles (George et al. 2007). This is akin to putting the Jack Welchs or Steve Jobs of the world under a microscope to find their commonalities so they can be emulated and replicated by the leaders in training. The cookie-cutter leadership approach would render future leaders ineffective as their individual unique strengths, voices, and experiences are ignored or suppressed. Instead, they are trapped in a canned approach to leadership, turning them into a replica or a better version of someone else.

The road to authentic leadership is entirely different. While studying patterns of leadership traits and behaviors of past and current leaders are of immense benefits, the lessons learned should be allowed to simmer in the chambers of one's minds and hearts for a while. This would allow the lessons learned to be intertwined with, tested against, and refined by his or her own inner voice, life experiences, new ideas. More often than not, the entire process will morph into something that is more customized to the individual.

Extant literature has distinguished authentic self from other concepts pertinent to self such as self-concept, self-esteem, self-presentation, self-monitoring, and self-serving bias. To review variants of what is now known as multidimensional and hierarchical models of self in relation to authentic self is simply beyond the scope of this chapter. It is important however to distinguish authenticity from sincerity as the

© Springer International Publishing Switzerland 2015

S. Sendjaya, *Personal and Organizational Excellence through Servant Leadership*, Management for Professionals, DOI 10.1007/978-3-319-16196-9_4 two have been often confused with each other in the popular press (Erickson 1995). Sincerity refers to the extent to which one's thoughts and feelings are accurately expressed to others (Trilling 1972). The point of reference is therefore someone outside oneself. Authenticity on other hand concerns with the commitment to be true to oneself in the absence of any reference to others. Inauthenticity therefore is the commitment to hide and/or alienate from oneself. Given its self-referential nature, authenticity is therefore much more intricate to understand.

Luthans and Avolio (2003) proposed a multi-dimensional construct of authentic leadership on the basis of conceptual roots in positive psychology. Focusing on self-awareness and self-regulatory processes, they define authentic leadership as a leadership behavior that nurtures and fosters a sense of self-awareness, an internalized moral perspective, balanced processing of information, and relational transparency (Walumbwa et al. 2008, p. 94). Shamir and Eilam (2005) proposed a narrower description of an authentic leader based on four attributes. First, authentic leaders stay true to themselves, enacting leadership role with or without a formal title (i.e., person-role merger). Second, authentic leaders are driven by convictions rather than self-centered benefits and agenda (i.e., self-concept clarity). Third, authentic leaders are originals, not replicas or mini-me version of someone, able and ready to offer their unique strength and perspective (i.e., self-concordant goals). Fourth, the consistency between their behavior and their self-concept, values and convictions (i.e., self-expression).

The above theorizing is helpful for an accurate understanding of authenticity in the authentic leadership theory. The *Authentic Self* dimension of servant leadership however is distinct. To develop and embody an authentic self, I argue that we need to understand the stark contrast between true self and false self and examine the three variants of false self, namely multiple selves, part-selves, and role-based self. When we fully grasp that an authentic self is not a false self, we are best placed to examine the five themes or values pertinent to the leader's authentic self.

4.1 False Self

The notion of authentic self has a long history in psychology, but it was quite distinct from the aforementioned contemporary applications of *authentic self* into the field of authentic leadership. Psychologist William James (1892) initially proposed that there are two conceptually distinct but experientially interrelated dimensions of self, the I-self and the Me-self. The I-self is the self-as-subject, the active observer, or the constructor whereas the Me-self is the self-as-object, the product of the observing process, the constructed. Cooley (1902) in contrast to James' cognitive-evaluative model, developed the looking-glass self, that is the self as a social construction based on perceptions of the evaluations that significant others have towards the self.

In its development, the theory of self in the 1960s evolved into the theorizing of true self and false self (Winnicott 1960). True self is the spontaneously real self that draws on holistic and transcendent presence within oneself. False self is the socially compliant self who artificially reacting to others' expectations in a treadmill of performance. As delineated above, at the core of false self is the incessant necessity to hide who they really are from others. Often it is accompanied by a strong feeling that others' acceptance and love will dramatically drop if they find out about the things meticulously kept in the hidden closet. As such, Harter et al. (1996, p. 360) defined false self behavior as "the extent to which one is acting in ways that do not reflect one's true self as a person".

Loss of voice has been singled out as a predominant manifestation of false self behavior (et al. 1997). This entails the inability to voice one's opinion or say what one really meant (e.g., "I tend to say one thing even when I think another"). Based on previous studies by Harter et al. (1997) and others on the loss of voice and self-silencing, Weir and Jose (2010) developed a false self scale that captures a wider range of false self beliefs and behaviors. Two additional dimensions that were added to signify false and true self are appearance/presentation and emotion/feeling. Appearance reveals false self behavior when one dresses to impress rather than to express one's own style, or to project a certain image commensurate with social expectations. (e.g., "I don't like to look different from other people"). False self behavior can also manifest in our efforts to hide one's true emotions. Specifically, negative internal feelings are suppressed and positive feelings are instead projected (e.g., "I hide my true feelings if I think they will upset others"). While this duplicity may create a certain level of psychological discomfort, the cost is outweighed by the threat of vulnerability resulting from being completely honest with one's feelings.

On the basis of the above theorizing of true self and false self, there are several distinct ways to construct false self that many leaders have been unknowingly fall victim of. That's probably why the path to become authentic leaders a treacherous one.

4.1.1   Multiple Selves

The construction of false self can emerge from the social necessity of having multiple roles concurrently. Harter (1988) contends that not all contradictions in self-concept are perceived as false self behavior as we need to act differently across different situations as part of our true self. That is, we experience multiple selves across different contexts as part of a normal socialization process. One may play different personas in the roles of a leader, follower, colleague, spouse, parent, board member, and volunteer, etc.

While the proliferation of selves is an evitable social reality for many, it can be challenging to maintain a coherent sense of self particularly in the presence of contradictory attributes in different roles (e.g., a team leader who has to be tough and direct with his team members at work, but gentle and nurturing to his children at home). The more investment one makes in ensuring that each of multiple selves conforms to expectations and demands in each relational context, the more complex the challenge to maintain authentic feelings and behaviors across different domains, leading one to live a saturated self (Gergen 1991). In the words of former Medtronic CEO Bill George and his colleagues (2007, p. 137): "Think of your life as a house, with a bedroom for your personal life, a study for your professional life, a family room for your family, and a living room to share with your friends. Can you knock down the walls between these rooms and be the same person in each of them?"

4.1.2 Part-Selves

False self is also nurtured when one suppresses the unwanted part selves that do not fit the projected image of self. Rather than disappearing, these part selves simply congregate as the hidden self, and we pretend that they do not exist. This is quite distinct from the aforementioned multiple selves arising out of our varied roles.

To acknowledge that life demands and social expectations often turn us into a fragmented rather than a single, coherent self is quite challenging. A leader with strong convictions and passion, for example, may also be an opinionated, patronizing, and insecure leader. If the leader is only aware of his competent self and never admits his abrasive and insecure self, he would be compelled to hide those unwanted parts behind his strong convictions. Refusing to face his insecure side would prompt the leader to live an illusion of effectiveness. Rather than accepting the unpleasant truth of his insecurity and fear, often such leader would erect a defensive wall by rationalizing or denying responsibility for his behavior.

Or consider a team leader who hides her contempt towards one of her team members because she fully realizes that her personal success partially depends on the expertise and experience of that team member. In so doing, she takes a step toward a loss of awareness of what he is really feeling. Instead she learns to fake her feeling and attitudes, appearing to comply with the person and ignoring the evidence to the contrary.

Since appearing, speaking, and reacting authentically can threaten one's self, we adjust our appearances, opinions and emotions to comply with social expectations. Thus, the belief that we can secure acceptance and acknowledgement by presenting ourselves in the most flattering light makes our lives feel like running in a treadmill of performance Slowly the masks that we put on to avoid feelings of vulnerability are becoming an integral part of our social self. Settling for a life of pretense, a truly authentic self becomes illusory. The quest to be authentic, therefore, involves encountering and embracing fragments of one's self that used to be unwanted. One's sociable side, playful self, ambitious self, temperamental self, cautious side, and many other facets of self are part and parcel of who one is.

4.1.3 Role-Based Self

Classic studies such as Zimbardo's Stanford Prison experiment and Milgram's obedience experiment among others show how lethal role internalization changes us to be someone completely different that who we really are (Zimbardo 2007). In much less dramatic contexts than those in social experiments, we possess in our normal lives a similar proclivity to allow our professional roles to define us.

This tendency can be observed during self-introduction in a common social function where mentioning our formal work titles and the ensuing response would determine our perceived self-worth. Thus, introducing ourselves as individuals with impressive positions in multinational companies will increase our esteem. Typically the conversation progresses into specific past achievements or future endeavors within the role to secure the image one is keen to project. On the contrary, admitting that we are still in-between jobs in the last 12 months would feel quite threatening. This otherwise menial social gesture speaks volume that our identity is often based on what we do rather than who we are.

Once leaders rely on their professional roles to define who they are, they typically engage in strategies to meet their needs for survival, acceptance, and control pertinent to those positions of power. Leaders can behave in abrasive and patronizing manner when challenged by their direct reports to hide their anxiety and insincerity. Or mask their indifference with surface level sympathy and colloquial. There are countless scenarios where they hone these skills for preservation or elevation purposes. As confirmed in Weir and Jose's (2010) study of false self manifestation, projecting a positive, socially desirable demeanor to hide a negative emotion is a type of false self behavior.

This presentation of self in the best possible light is designed to create a favorable, context-appropriate impression. While accomplishing these things are quite legitimate indicators of leadership success, and as such is not problematic in and of itself, the leader's increasing reliance on these professional accomplishments and qualities in defining themselves turn them into a different self. Since an inordinate investment of the leaders' time, attention, and energy is required to build and maintain this image and way of being, they increasingly become adept at the art of packaging self through hiding and pretending. The subtlest impact of this cacophony of false pretension however lies in the shift in how they see themselves. The mask they manufacture initially reflects how they want others to perceive them but over time they become reflection of how they want to see themselves. In other words, they initially create a mask then the mask creates them. The false self they pretend to be subtly merges with, engulfs, and overpowers their original self, morphing it into something else. Often what they claim as 'authentic' is actually a new identity assumed by the leaders.

In summary at the core of the false self is the inordinate desire to preserve a façade of self that gives us a perceived sense of internal security. The false self we spent many years building up and becoming holds us captive as we are fixated with others' perceptions towards us. We continue to hide some aspects of ourselves in dark corners for fear of being exposed.

Granted there is a reason why we are called human beings rather than human doings. We are not our achievements. We are not our roles. The things we can do or have done ought not define us. Our worth lies in who we are as human beings, not what we can do, have done, or how others see us. Like the proverbial peeled onion, if our layer after layer of the inauthentic self is stripped away, what eventually remains is the naked, authentic self.

4.2   Authentic Self

Unlike animals or plants, humans with the complex functioning of their internal apparatus always feel the urge to pursue false ways of being. A cat does not feel the need to appear or behave like a horse, and a Royal Gala apple tree will never attempt to dress up like a Golden Delicious tree. An authentic self is a true self rather than a pretense, superficial self. Being authentic in the final analysis is about knowing and being who we really are (Autry 2001).

How can we tell if someone is truly authentic? What does authenticity look like? What are the observable behaviors which signify authenticity? My research in this area suggests that there are five values of authenticity that are essential to servant leadership. Indeed the need and importance of authentic functioning in leader-follower relationships has been acknowledged in the literature (De Pree 1989). A servant leader manifests an authentic self when he or she is humble, integrated, accountable, secure, and vulnerable. In other words, the extent to which a servant leader is authentic hinges on the following sub-dimensions or attributes: humility, integrity, accountability, security, and vulnerability.

Since their leadership flows out of 'being', servant leaders are capable of leading authentically as manifested in their consistent display of the aforementioned five indicators. In practical terms, this means that knowing and being who they really are, servant leaders practice what they preach, admit their mistakes and limitations, and are not defensive when their decisions and actions are questioned. In contrast to insecure leaders who 'operate with a deep, unexamined insecurity about their own identity', servant leaders are able to work behind the scenes willingly without constant acknowledgement or approval from others. Their secure sense of self enables them to be accountable and vulnerable to others, marked by the absence of self-defensiveness when criticized.

4.2.1   Humility

Humility have increasingly become a subject of interest in the context of leadership as endless corporate scandals often caused or exacerbated by untamed ego, hubris, arrogance, and self-entitlement manifested by countless corporate executives. In other words, the absence of humility is key to understanding this global phenomenon of corporate demise. Leaders who are full of themselves would have a hard time practicing servant leadership since becoming a servant leader means emptying one's self to the humble service of others. A comprehensive review of the humility literature is well documented in the literature (see, for example, Exline and Geyer 2004; Tangney 2000).

Humility is a key virtue in many philosophical and religious teachings. Immanuel Kant for example conceptualized humility as a "meta-attitude which constitutes the moral agent's proper perspective on himself" that underlies other virtues such as courage, wisdom, and compassion (Grenberg 2005, p. 133). In the Judeo-Christian tradition, humility is defined as "the sense of entire nothingness, which comes when we see how truly God is all, and in which we make way for God to be all" (Murray 1982, p. 12). In Taoism, humility is considered by Lao Tzu as a non-negotiable essential for leadership effectiveness: "I have three precious things which I hold fast and prize. The first is gentleness; the second is frugality; the third is humility, which keeps me from putting myself before others. Be gentle and you can be bold; be frugal and you can be liberal; avoid putting yourself before others and you can become a leader among men" (Tzu 2008, p. 24). Foster (1989, p. 163) observed the peculiarity of humility as a virtue: "Humility is one of those virtues that is never gained by seeking it. The more we pursue it the more distant it becomes. To think we have it is sure evidence that we don't."

Unfortunately a long held misconception that humility signifies an inferior sense of worth or low self-esteem or personal weakness (Morris et al. 2005), and a host of negative attitudes such as "shyness, lack of ambition, passivity, or lack of confidence" (Vera and Rodriguez-Lopez 2004, p. 393) is still quite popular today. Contrary to these views, humility essentially refers to the idea of making a right estimation of one's self. Granted the process of rightly estimating one's self necessitates a right understanding of one's self. Humility therefore negates the non-overestimation or under-estimation of one's standing.

Fast forward two and a half thousand years, and we find that modern leadership studies scientifically confirm the views of the aforementioned ancient writers on humility. Collins' (2001) 5-year study on companies that made extraordinary transformations revealed that the organizational leaders of successful companies embody personal humility. While humility is not singled out as the only attribute that characterizes the leaders of the good-to-great companies, it is a virtue that is clearly associated with effective leadership. Some of the behavioral attitudes identified in the study include acting quietly without deliberately seeking public adulation, attributing the organizational success to factors other outside themselves, and admitting readily to others their limitations (Collins 2001). When the leader is not worried about who gets the credit for work well done, he or she is able to do things without constant approval and recognition from others (Bennis and Nanus 1985). The following comment from a CEO of an accounting software development firm from my interview study brings home the point:

> [Humility] is recognizing that as a leader you are still one person. That if something is going well, it's not because you're such a hero... In fact, if you're genuinely leading as a servant then you will reward or pass on the reward to those that have contributed to that result. Even though others might choose to see you as the hero. You'd rather deflect that to others that have done the work even if you've been involved in it.

These comments show that humility occurs when leaders give credit to external factors and other people for success, and deflect recognition of themselves to others. That personal humility is shown when leaders shun attention and deflect recognition is also confirmed in Badaracco's (2002) research among corporate executives. He found that suggested that humble leaders work quietly, carefully, and patiently behind the scenes. Their willingness to spend time on small things and make seemingly inconsequential decisions unrewarded and unnoticed is an indication of their modesty. Their modest outlook on themselves prevents them from being defensive when confronted, and boastful when praised. In fact they are quite reluctant to think about their own leadership legacy as this executive from a large charity organization remarks:

> It becomes too hard if you start thinking about legacies because then you become too self-absorbed about creating an environment where you'd be remembered. And I think that's self-defeating in this industry. I'm actually very proud of working for this organization because I know that my effort will truly save millions of lives every year. But if I become self-absorbed in creating an environment where in a few years time they will say, "Joe Bloke did that", it goes against what I stand for. Therefore, I am honestly not worried or even think about that. I think for today as long I am doing a good job.

More recently, in their efforts to operationalize the construct of humility, Owen et al. (2013, p. 1518) defined humility as an interpersonal characteristic that emerges in social contexts that connotes (a) a manifested willingness to view oneself accurately, (b) a displayed appreciation of others' strengths and contributions, and (c) teachability. These behavioral attributes fit well with the servant leadership philosophy. It would be incredibly hard for any leader to exercise the three strands of humility if they do not have a servant heart, for they require the leaders to put others' opinions and perceptions before those of themselves. American philosopher Ralph W. Emerson captured this sentiment when he wrote, "In my walks, every man I meet is my superior in some way, and in that I learn from him." First, servant leaders are willing to see themselves accurately through learning and gaining insights from their interactions with others. The people they work with become social mirrors through which they can present their authentic selves. The goal however is not only to make sense of self but also modify the self whenever appropriate, hence their self-concept is derived interdependent rather than independent of others (Nielsen et al. 2010). As such, they never dread self-disclosure, when appropriate willingly become transparent about their limitations, faults, and mistakes. The courage to show their followers they are not infallible includes admitting personal foibles, knowledge gaps, lapses in judgment, and bad decisions as well as taking a full responsibility for failures or losing control of their emotions. As such, 'sorry' is not the hardest word for them to say, instead they would be quick to admit that they do not have all the answers. 'I apologize' and 'That's my fault' are part of their everyday lingo. In their article, Owen and Hekman (2012, p. 794) cited an interviewee's comment as follows: "Humility gives us the ability, not only to recover quickly when we are getting too emotional but to allow other people to know, "Hey, I just have to let you know hat I need to step aside for a moment or you need to have a little patience with me right now, because I'm not myself.""

Second, servant leaders are adept at identifying and affirming followers' strengths and talents rather than feeling threatened by their superior intelligence and talents. This implies that servant leaders have a strong valuation of others, without a declining valuation of self. In the words of Max DePree (1989, p. 16), Chairman and CEO of Herman Miller, Inc., a servant leader would "abandon oneself to the strength of others." Leaders would frequently encourage followers to come forward with ideas to improve any facet of the corporate life, and properly reward such contributions. In the course of doing so, servant leaders become students of the followers' strengths and deflect recognitions that people give onto their followers. Driven by the belief that 'none of us is as smart as all of us', they would be reluctant to appear as the ultimate authority who have the final say in everything.

Finally, the humility of servant leaders is also shown in their teachability. Servant leaders are teachable because they have a deep awareness of their own fallibility and thus need other people to remind and show them their blind spots. Each of us has blind spots. However, given the authority and power attached to leadership positions, it is easy for leaders to be defensive, particularly towards unsolicited feedback from followers. Each of us carries within ourselves an inner lawyer whom we can activate at will to rise to our defense. And seasoned leaders are known to carry fierce and aggressive attorneys! Often these counselors begin a silent defense of ourselves the minute someone is respectfully pointing out a single blemish in us. Before the person even finish showing evidence of a need for change on our behalf, we erect mounting evidence that we are not the person they think we are. Servant leaders fire these inner lawyers because they instinctively know that they need others as much as others need them to change and grow into what they are capable of becoming. This self-awareness manifests in their approachability and willingness to consider others' inputs as the background noise of their inner defense systems slowly subsides. By being teachable, servant leaders progressively grow in self-knowledge, allowing them to remain authentic in the truest sense of the word.

4.2.2 Integrity

Integrity has been singled out as an intangible strategic asset for both individual leaders and organizations (Petrick and Quinn 2001). The lack of credibility even in some of the most respected government, business, and not-for-profit organizations is often attributed to the vanishing integrity of the leaders. The word integrity comes from the Latin integritas which means wholeness or completeness. Its root word integer means intact or untouched. Integrity implies a life that is well integrated marked by a coherence among its different parts. It is shown most clearly in what one would do if he or she would never be found out.

That integrity is one of the key attributes of servant leadership has been well documented (Russell and Stone 2002; Sendjaya et al. 2008; Wong and Page 2003). Servant leaders who lead with integrity do not live a life of duplicity or hypocrisy because they have nothing to hide or fear and their lives are open books. They are who they are no matter where they are or who they are with. There is no discrepancy between their public and private lives or their professional and personal lives. A simple self-reflection on the two following questions would test the integrity of a leader: "What kind of person do most people think you are?" and "How do you think you really are?" The bigger the gap between the two answers would suggest that one is more concerned with image (what people think we are) rather than integrity (what we really are). Servant leaders who focus on integrity-building are true to themselves in both big and small ways. They would never engage in bribery, fraud, or character assassination but they would also be punctual if they expect their followers to be punctual or treating people with the same courteous manner publicly and privately. As such, their followers never have to second-guess the leaders because there is a consistent pattern in what the leaders believe and how they would act. Servant leaders will not hold their followers to a higher standard than the one they hold for themselves.

A second and more commonly understood meaning of integrity in the literature is word and deed consistency. Simon (1990, p. 90) defines behavioral integrity as "the perceived degree of congruence between the values expressed by words and those expressed through actions." The perceived level of integrity of an individual is a manifestation of a commitment to principled behavior in accordance with his or her personal values or principles, particularly in the presence of temptation or challenge to do the contrary (Badaracco and Ellsworth 1989). The absence of competing value systems and beliefs within one's self is the prerequisite of personal integrity, which is critical for leaders and leadership effectiveness (Kouzes and Posner 1995). Hence, living with integrity entails a life reflecting one's conviction and being true to one's self (Worden 2003). When their words and deeds are aligned, servant leaders show their lives are 'in sync' as aptly illustrated in the following story of baby Zoe told by her grandfather (DePree 1992, p. 1)

> She was born prematurely and weighed only one pound, seven ounces, so small that my wedding ring could slide up her arm to her shoulder. The neonatologist who first examined her told us that she had a 5 to 10 % chance of living three days . . . To complicate matters, Zoe's biological father had jumped ship the month before Zoe was born. Realizing this, a wise and caring nurse named Ruth gave me my instructions: "For the next several months, at least, you're the surrogate father. I want you to come to the hospital everyday to visit Zoe, and when you come, I would like you to rub her body and her legs and her arms with the tip of your finger. While you're caressing her, you should tell her over and over again how much you love her, because she has to be able to connect your voice to your touch."

The lesson DePree drew from that personal experience for leaders is the importance of always connecting one's voice and one's touch. Simons (2002) notes the distinction between the actual or perceived alignment of words and deeds in under-standing behavioral integrity. Given the subjective nature of behavioral integrity, it is important for servant leaders not only manifests actual word-deed consistency but also communicate what they think, feel, or believe behind what is seen and observed, lest the followers fail to perceive the congruence between the leaders' values and actions. For example, servant leaders need to be transparent about the real reasons behind the decisions they make, or take ownership for the broken promise without making excuses or apologies. Practically speaking, servant leaders demonstrate integrity when they choose to stay true to their principles rather than being popular, speak honestly even if that means they would lose something of value, following through their commitments and honoring their promises irrespective of the cost. The absence of these behaviors indicates the loss of integrity which most definitely would lead to the loss of leadership authority. Unfortunately this is often the case in the corporate world as lamented by a director of a leadership training organization as follows:

> A classic example, this morning you might have heard it on the news, that the senior executive of an Australian bank who some time ago made all this grand statement about senior executives getting paid too much and all these options were bad things. It's just been revealed that he's been receiving one and a half million dollars in options and other things. Total hypocrisy . . . If the majority of senior executives in this country are only there to line their own pockets, in the end we're in big trouble. Because you cannot build the social capital of a country, indeed you can't even build the economic capital of the country, probably, if that's the sort of leadership you have . . . That's why I think the concept of servant leader is so important. And a lot of people talk the talk but they don't walk the walk.

4.2.3   Accountability

Leaders who are built to last rather than to flip would need accountability. Just like a scale reveals how effective one has been in working out his or her new year's resolutions on exercise and diet, accountability shows leaders' intentionality and consistency in maintaining their effectiveness. Accountability helps leaders guard themselves against follies that can render their leadership ineffective or destructive. No one drifts into becoming excellent, effective, and efficient leaders. It takes more than one person to create such leaders.

Unfortunately accountability is often misunderstood in one of the following ways. First, it is a blame-shifting exercise inflicted upon someone when something goes wrong. Second, it is a regular reporting of mistakes and wrongdoings already committed to senior management. Third, it is a public confession of something one would otherwise keep private. Little wonder why many leaders avoid making themselves answerable to others. While accountability assumes taking ownership of the decisions or actions that one does, its main purpose is not absorbing the blame or creating excuse to soften the damage but to ensure that one's leadership effectiveness remains at its highest possible level. Accountability also does not entail providing total access and full authority for everyone to probe into the leaders' lives both professionally and personally. Rather as Swindoll (1989, p. 126) suggests, accountability is "opening one's life to a few carefully selected, trusted, loyal confidants who speak the truth – who have the right to examine, to question, to appraise, and to give counsel."

Servant leaders not only accept accountability as a principle but seeking it willingly because as Marshall (1991, p. 72) outlines:

> Servants like to be accountable, they are accustomed to being answerable for their performance because they want to know whether they have satisfactorily met the requirements of those they serve. It is not the natural inclination of leaders to want to be accountable. Their tendency is more in the direction of independence and freedom of action, thus the attitude of leaders towards accountability and answerability is often a good indication as to whether they have the heart of true servanthood.

Critics of servant leadership are quick to point out that applying servant leadership is risky because the leaders will be treated like a doormat, expected to do what they are asked and take the fall when things go south. Their service orientation is often manipulated or taken for granted by others. But the following comment from a research organization director suggests otherwise:

> Call it 'I am your servant, but you are not my master'. . . If you think servant leadership is just giving the people what they want . . . you are actually missing the generous nature of true servant leadership. Your relative accountability is to the people you work with and who work for you. So you do have a relative accountability then, but it's not absolute.

Block (1993) echoed a similar view arguing that servant leaders view themselves as stewards who hold themselves accountable for the well-being and growth of the people they serve. In order to be accountable, servant leaders choose a number of individuals to question their actions and decisions to provide honest, candid feedback. They take personal responsibility for decisions collectively made, and are committed to meet the expectations of those people they serve. Barrs (1983, pp. 47–48) maintained that leaders who put themselves on an unrealistic pedestal without any accountability mechanism are bound to fail:

> We may be given different positions of responsibility and authority . . ., but never does our position set us apart from our fellow human beings. We must always therefore be ready for our behavior and decisions to be questioned, discussed, and criticized. We must be open to correction and rebuke.

In the absence of accountability, leaders will gather around them blind followers who carry out orders given to them uncritically (i.e., yes-men and women) or alienated followers who make it their mission to point out every single negative area in the leader while overlooking the positive ones. Gardner (1990, p. 135) aptly captures it, "Pity the leader who is caught between unloving critics and uncritical lovers. Leaders need reassurance, but just as important they need advisors who tell them the truth, gently but candidly." While the overwhelming majority of leaders might prefer dishonest followers who praise rather than indifferent followers who criticize, given enough time they both will render leaders ineffective. As such, rather than surrounding themselves with unloving critics or uncritical lovers, servant leaders help transforming them into *critical lovers* who will tell the hard truth in a loving manner. Bennis (1994, p. xxii) echoed the same sentiment when he remarked:

> Nothing will sink a leader faster than surrounding him- or herself with yes-men and women. Even when principled nay-sayers are wrong, they force leaders to re-evaluate their positions and to poke and prod their assumptions for weaknesses. Good ideas are only made stronger by being challenged.

Accountability is terribly needed because leaders are prone to self-deception, perhaps more so than average human beings given the status and prestige often associated with leadership positions. Our capacity to deceive ourselves is much greater than our capacity to deceive others. We are quite adept at identifying self-deception in others. We can detect if someone tried to rationalize their socially unacceptable behaviors. But recognizing these same things in ourselves is much more difficult. Self-deception occurs in endlessly creative and instinctive ways.

In summary, accountability is an effective safeguard to avoid an elitist culture where one or a few individuals dominate the organization. Servant leaders therefore do not just passively wait for inputs and feedback from others, they actively solicit them. In fact, being fully aware of followers' reluctance of providing negative feedback for fear of the consequences, servant leaders would give followers the right to question the actions and decisions they are about to commit themselves into. They issue their followers a hunting license to catch a glimpse of character flaw or lapse in judgement on their part and call for an honest look-you-in-the-eye conversation.

Accountability Exercise
Ask these eight questions in your accountability group to hold each other accountable. Doing it regularly would help maintain your leadership edge sharp.

1. Are you consciously or unconsciously creating the impression you are better than you really are? Do you tend to exaggerate what you have said or done?
2. Do you grumble and complain constantly? Are you self-pitying or self-justifying?
3. Are you a slave to image, appearance, work, or certain habits?
4. Have you recently compromise your integrity in your financial dealings?
5. Have you given priority time to your family? To your personal growth?
6. Has your productivity been badly affected by someone you fear, dislike, criticize, or hold resentment toward? If so, what will you do about it?
7. Have you hurt someone verbally, either behind their back or face-to-face?
8. Have you been completely honest with me, or have you just lied to me?

4.2.4 Security

Palmer (1998) argued that many leaders have a deep insecurity about their own identity and self-worth. More often than not their identity is tightly attached to external roles and responsibilities. These insecure leaders are so dependent on the external world that they would not be able to function properly in the absence of these roles and positions. In fact, their insecure sense of self causes negative consequences in others, or in Palmer's words (1998, p. 202): "When leaders operate with a deep, unexamined insecurity about their own identity, they create institutional settings that deprive other people of their identity as a way of dealing with the unexamined fears in the leaders themselves."

The servant leader's deliberate choice to serve and be a servant should not be associated with any forms of low self-concept or self-image, in the same way as choosing to forgive should not be viewed as a sign of weakness. Instead, it would take a leader with an accurate understanding of his or her self-image, moral conviction and emotional stability to make such a choice. Servant leaders' secure sense of self enables them to work behind the scenes willingly without acknowledgement or approval from others, to distribute their power and authority to others without hesitation, and to step aside for more qualified successors without feeling threatened.

An example of such secure servant leaders is Jesus Christ, who "did not consider equality with God something to be grasped, but made himself nothing, taking the very nature of a servant" (NIV Bible, Philippians 2:3–8). Commenting on the story of Jesus washed his disciples' feet, Ford (1991) points out that it was not weakness that compelled Jesus to be a servant in this case. Instead, it was a sense of being deeply secure in his identity that moved Jesus to make a deliberate sacrifice of himself. Firmly anchored in their self-identity, servant leaders deliberately serve others, share their authority with others, and distribute their power to others. The following interview comment illustrate the attribute of *Security*:

> Another point I have is that servant leadership requires a degree of emotional and psychological and spiritual health on the part of a leader. Unhealthy leaders, and by that I mean leaders who are very insecure or driven by some of the dark sides inside themselves, will find themselves struggling to do servant leadership because to serve others rather than exercise power over them requires an internal security. If you haven't got an internal security, or a reasonable level of it, none of us is a hundred percent secure unless you've got a reasonable level of internal security, you'll find servant leadership hard.

4.2.5 Vulnerability

While vulnerability has not traditionally been linked to leadership, it is always considered a key servant leadership quality. Autry (2001) contends that in the workplace context servant leaders display vulnerability when they are honest with their feelings and open with their doubts and concerns about someone's or their own performance. Servant leaders do not have hesitations to say to their followers "I don't know" or "I was wrong", and are open about their own limitations and shortcomings. In fact, for servant leaders the absence of defensiveness is an indication of strength and maturity (Batten 1998). Servant leaders are more focused towards being fruitful over and above being successful. While they appreciate that control, achievements, and strengths breed personal and organizational success but these tangible indicators are impotent to create a deep, genuine leader-follower relationship. Nouwen (1997) noted that just like a child is the fruit conceived in vulnerability and a community is the fruit born through shared brokenness, the intimacy between leaders and followers are sown through touching one another's wounds.

Servant leaders are well aware of the positive leadership effects brought about by vulnerability. First, admission of a weakness fosters support and collaboration. When leaders project an image that they are flawless, they imply that they are better off without others on board. On the contrary, when leaders admit a weakness, they demonstrate to people that they are fallible and limited, and need the participation of others to succeed. In the words of DePree (1997, p. 182): "Vulnerable leaders are open to the diversity of gifts from followers. They seek contrary opinion. They take every person seriously. They are strong enough to abandon themselves to the strengths of others."

Second, sharing an imperfection builds solidarity between leaders and followers since followers can identify themselves with leaders who openly declare that they are prone to errors (Goffee and Jones 2000). The leaders' frankness about their limitations indicates their humanity, approachability and authenticity, which are positively perceived by the followers. Such identification is much harder to achieve with leaders who always try to prove that they are infallible and spotless.

Third, voluntarily disclosing a weakness prevents others to invent one for the leaders (Bain and Loader 1998). Exposing oneself to the experience of vulnerability allows the leader to be open to new learning, growth, and opportunity. Owen and Hekman (2012) however issued a caveat emptor on self-admission of faults, highlighting that its effectiveness hinges upon followers' perception of the leaders competence. In the absence of a reputation for competence, personal transparency becomes a risky venture and can seriously undermine followers' competence-based trust on the leaders.

Autry (2001, p. 15), however, observed that being vulnerable is not as straight-forward as most leaders think:

> Being vulnerable takes a great deal of courage because it means letting go of the old notions of control, forgetting forever the illusion that you can be in control. Too many of us think that our powers come from your ability to maintain control. To the contrary, our power comes from realizing that we can't be in control and that we must depend on others.

The following interview comment from a CEO illustrates vulnerability in practical terms:

> [Servant leadership] is scary. Because you must be more vulnerable. You have to earn people's willingness to follow you. It's not like imposing your will on people or controlling people. And often very controlling leaders, very authoritarian leaders are actually very insecure. That's why they operate like that. If you have a servant-type leader, then he or she will be open to criticism and allow a vice president of heresy. Someone who's willing to sort of say the outlandish thing and say, "Look, you know. The product we're making is crap or something like that, you know … We're not doing a good job. We really need to fix this up." And you need to allow that sort of communication channel to be in place. Leaders who encourage that climate will have better organizations.

Finally, vulnerability allows leaders to protect themselves from their own wounds, and heal others who suffer from similar wounds. Everyone brings primal baggage from their past to work, then operate at work with their desires and neuroses– be it a desire for attention, approval, achievement, or control. Rather than perceiving reality as they are, people view it through the lens of these wounds (e.g., unfulfilled desires, unresolved hurts). Goodman (2007) argued that wounded executives typically become simultaneously the most productive yet the most toxic leaders. Driven by the hunger for attention and approval, they perform solo at their peak performance to the top often to the detriment of their soul. Meanwhile given the unspoken expectation in the organization that leaders must be woundless entity, the wounds force them to split off certain parts of themselves. Vulnerability allows leaders to have their wounds nursed by others, and only when those wounds are healed can they be wounder healers for others. Nouwen (1972, p. 72) aptly captures this notion of leaders as wounded healers in the following comments:

> After so much stress on the necessity of a leader to prevent his own personal feelings and attitudes from interfering in a helping relationship . . . it seems necessary to re-establish the basic principle that none can help anyone without becoming involved without entering with his whole person into the painful situation, without taking the risk of becoming hurt, wounded or even destroyed in the process. The beginning and the end of all . . . leadership is to give your life for others . . . [this] starts with the willingness to cry with those who cry, laugh with those who laugh, and *to make one's own painful and joyful experiences available as sources of clarification and understanding.*

4.3   Actionable Commitments of Servant Leadership

The following actionable commitments are associated with the five values of the *Authentic Self* dimension. They have been validated in multiple studies as part of the 35-item servant leadership behavior scale (SLBS), hence can be implemented with confidence in different settings and cultures.

Commitment #8 – Avoid being defensive when confronted
What do people say or do that would make you angry? Examining when and where your ego hurts is a useful exercise to practice humility. It is quite typical for a leader with a strong conviction to be very opinionated, feel superior, and non-teachable. Remember it was pride that turned an angel into the devil, thus before it leads you into the same path, handle confrontation with care and let it illuminate the dark corners of your false self.

Commitment #9 – When criticized, focus on the message not the messenger
As every seasoned leader would know, being a leader at times feels like painting a target on your back and inviting people to open fire at you. But servant leaders know that criticism will ruin their souls more than their reputations. It indulges them in self-pity then tempts them to shoot the critic. Instead of doing that, try to find a kernel of truth in even the most unfair, exaggerated, or mistaken comment. The critic could be partially right for the wrong reasons, thus do not dismiss that opportunity for have an honest look at yourself, then respond accordingly.

Commitment #10 – Practice what you preach
Do you follow through what you promise? Do you personally role model the behaviors you want others to exhibit? Do you make your unedited thoughts known to others? Even the worst tyrants get an enormous respect from their followers because of the consistency between their words and deeds. On the contrary, a servant leader with a grand vision, deep conviction, and superb articulation but no integration of words and deeds will be in due time perceived as a fraud.

Commitment #11 – Give others the right to question my actions and decisions
If people in your inner circle are reluctant to question or challenge you, they either become yes people or talk behind your back. To avoid this huge disadvantage, you should verbally and repeatedly give the permission to speak to you freely and gently. That hunting license you issue them will save you from a lot of trouble that comes mostly from yourself.

Commitment #12 – Let others take control of situations when appropriate
A secure sense of self is evident if you are surrounded by people more talented than you and can trust them to take charge accordingly. You are not the expert in everything and your identity should be rooted on something more permanent than work performance that fluctuates.

Commitment #13 – Be willing to say "I was wrong" to other people
Vulnerability is a great asset for servant leaders, and humble admission of faults is an important way to grow it. Saying "I was wrong" has a much more positive impact than saying "I was right". This involves taking personal responsibility for the blunders made by your team.

References

Autry, J. A. (2001). *The servant leader*. Roseville: Prima.

Badaracco, J. L. (2002). *Leading quietly*. Boston: Harvard Business School Press.

Badaracco, J. L., & Ellsworth, R. R. (1989). *Leadership and the quest for integrity*. Boston: Harvard Business School Press.

Bain, A., & Loader, D. (1998). Leadership and vulnerability. *Incorporated Association of Registered Teachers of Victoria (IARTV) Occasional Papers, 54*, 1–7.

Barrs, J. (1983). *Shepherds and sheep: A biblical view of leading and following*. Downers Grove: InterVarsity Press.

Batten, J. (1998). Servant leadership: A passion to serve. In L. C. Spears (Ed.), *Insights on leadership: Service, stewardship, spirit, and servant leadership* (pp. 38–53). New York: Wiley.

Bennis, W. (1994). *On becoming a leader*. Reading: Addison-Wesley.

Bennis, W. G., & Nanus, B. (1985). *Leaders: The strategies for taking charge*. New York: Harper & Row.

Block, P. (1993). *Stewardship: Choosing service over self-interest*. San Francisco: Berrett Koehler.

Collins, J. (2001). Level 5 leadership: The triumph of humility and fierce resolve. *Harvard Business Review, 79*(1): 67–76.

Cooley, C. H. (1902). *Human nature and the social order*. New York: Scribner's.

De Pree, M. (1989). *Leadership is an art*. New York: Dell Publishing.

De Pree, M. (1997). *Leading without power: Finding hope in serving community.* San Francisco: Jossey-Bass.

DePree, M. (1992). *Leadership Jazz.* New York: Currency Doubleday.

Erickson, R. J. (1995). The importance of authenticity for self and society. *Symbolic Interaction, 18*(2), 121–144.

Exline, J. J., & Geyer, A. L. (2004). Perceptions of humility: A preliminary study. *Self and Identity, 3*, 95–114.

Ford, L. (1991). *Transforming leadership: Jesus' way of creating vision, shaping values and empowering change.* Downers Grove: InterVarsity Press.

Foster, R. J. (1989). *Celebration of discipline.* London: Hodder & Stoughton.

Gardner, J. (1990). *On leadership.* New York: Free Press.

George, B., Sims, P., McLean, A. N., & Mayer, D. (2007). Discovering your authentic leadership. *Harvard Business Review, 85*(2), 129–138.

Gergen, K. J. (1991). *The saturated self.* New York: Basic Books.

Goffee, R., & Jones, G. (2000). Why should anyone be led by you? *Harvard Business Review, 78*(5), 63–70.

Goodman, D. (2007). Leading with wounds: A liability or gift? *Journal for Religious Leadership, 5*(1), 39–69.

Grenberg, J. (2005). *Kant and the ethics of humility.* Cambridge: Cambridge University Press.

Harter, S. (1988). Developmental and dynamic changes in the nature of the self-concept. In *Cognitive development and child psychotherapy* (pp. 119–160). New York: Springer.

Harter, S., Marold, D. B., Whitesell, N., & Cobbs, G. (1996). A model of the effects of perceived parent and peer support on adolescent false self behavior. *Child Development, 67*(2), 360–374.

Harter, S., Waters, P. L., & Whitesell, N. R. (1997). Lack of voice as a manifestation of false self-behavior among adolescents: The school setting as a stage upon which the drama of authenticity is enacted. *Educational Psychologist, 32*, 153–173.

James, W. (1892). *Psychology: The briefer course.* New York: Henry Holt.

Kouzes, J. M., & Posner, B. Z. (1995). *The leadership challenge: How to keep getting extraordinary things done in organizations.* San Francisco: Jossey-Bass.

Luthans, F., & Avolio, B. J. (2003). Authentic leadership development. In K. S. Cameron, J. E. Dutton, & R. E. Quinn (Eds.), *Positive organizational scholarship* (pp. 241–258). San Francisco: Berrett-Koehler.

Marshall, T. (1991). *Understanding leadership: Fresh perspectives on the essentials of New Testament leadership.* Chichester: Sovereign World.

Morris, J. A., Brotheridge, C. M., & Urbanski, J. C. (2005). Bringing humility to leadership: Antecedents and consequences of leader humility. *Human Relations, 58*(10), 1323–1350.

Murray, A. (1982). *Humility.* New Kensington: Whitaker House.

Nielsen, R., Marrone, J. A., & Slay, H. S. (2010). A new look at humility: Exploring the humility concept and its roles in socialized charismatic leadership. *Journal of Leadership and Organizational Studies, 17*(1), 33–43.

Nouwen, H. J. M. (1972). *The wounded healer: Ministry in contemporary society.* New York: Doubleday.

Nouwen, H. (1997). *Bread for the journey: A daybook of wisdom and faith.* New York: HarperCollins.

Owens, B. P., & Hekman, D. R. (2012). Modeling how to grow: An inductive examination of humble leader behaviors, contingencies, and outcomes. *Academy of Management Journal, 55*, 787–818.

Owens, B. P., Johnson, M. D., & Mitchell, T. R. (2013). Expressed humility in organizations: Implications for performance, teams, and leadership. *Organization Science, 24*, 1517–1538.

Palmer, P. J. (1998). Leading from within. In L. C. Spears (Ed.), *Insights on leadership: Service, stewardship, spirit, and servant leadership* (pp. 197–208). New York: Wiley.

Petrick, J. A., & Quinn, J. F. (2001). The challenge of leadership accountability for integrity capacity as a strategic asset. *Journal of Business Ethics, 34*(3/4), 331–343.

Russell, R. F., & Stone, A. G. (2002). A review of servant leadership attributes: Developing a practical model. *Leadership & Organization Development Journal, 23*(3), 145–147.

Sendjaya, S., Sarros, J. C., & Santora, J. C. (2008). Defining and measuring servant leadership behaviour in organizations. *Journal of Management Studies, 45*(2), 402–424.

Shamir, B., & Eilam, G. (2005). "What's your story?" A life-stories approach to authentic leadership development. *The Leadership Quarterly, 16*(3), 395–417.

Simon, A. M. (1990). A generative research strategy for data production. Illustrated by a Zimbabwean and a South African case study. In P. Hugo (Ed.), *Truth be in the field.* Pretoria: UNISA.

Simons, T. (2002). Behavioral integrity: The perceived alignment between managers' words and deeds as a research focus. *Organization Science, 13*(1), 18–35.

Swindoll, C. R. (1989). *Living above the level of mediocrity.* Dallas: Word.

Tangney, J. P. (2000). Humility: Theoretical perspectives, empirical findings and directions for future research. *Journal of Social and Clinical Psychology, 19*, 70–82.

Trilling, L. (1972). *Sincerity and authenticity.* New York: Harcourt Brace Jovanovich.

Tzu, L. (2008). The sayings of Lao Tzu. Radford: Wilder Publications.

Vera, D., & Rodriguez-Lopez, A. (2004). Strategic virtues: Humility as a source of competitive advantage. *Organizational Dynamics, 33*(4), 393–408.

Walumbwa, F. O., Avolio, B. J., Gardner, W. L., Wernsing, T. S., & Peterson, S. J. (2008). Authentic leadership: Development and validation of a theory-based measure. *Journal of Management, 34*, 89–126.

Weir, K. F., & Jose, P. E. (2010). The perception of false self scale for adolescents: Reliability, validity, and longitudinal relationships with depressive and anxious symptoms. *British Journal of Developmental Psychology, 28*, 393–411.

Winnicott, D. W. (1960). Ego distortion in terms of true and false self. In *The maturational process and the facilitating environment: Studies in the theory of emotional development* (pp. 140–152). New York: International UP Inc.

Wong, P. T. P., & Page, D. (2003). *Servant leadership: An opponent-process model and the revised servant leadership profile.* Paper presented at the Servant Leadership Research Roundtable, Virginia Beach, VA.

Worden, S. (2003). The role of integrity as a mediator in strategic leadership: A recipe for reputational capital. *Journal of Business Ethics, 46*(1), 31–44.

Zimbardo, P. (2007). *The Lucifer effect: Understanding how good people turn evil.* New York: Random House.

Covenantal Relationship

5

> *To love at all is to be vulnerable. Love anything and your heart*
> *will be wrung and possibly broken. If you want to make sure of*
> *keeping it intact you must give it to no one, not even an animal.*
> *Wrap it carefully round with hobbies and little luxuries; avoid*
> *all entanglements. Lock it up safe in the casket or coffin of your*
> *selfishness. But in that casket, safe, dark, motionless, airless, it*
> *will change. It will not be broken; it will become unbreakable,*
> *impenetrable, irredeemable.*
>
> (C. S. Lewis, *The Four Loves*)

The third dimension of servant leadership, *Covenantal Relationship*, refers to a relationship of mutual commitment by individuals characterized by shared values, open-ended commitment, mutual trust, and concern for the welfare of the other party (Bromley and Busching 1988; De Pree 1989; Elazar 1980; Graham and Organ 1993). Covenants are intensely personal bonds of individuals who engage in intrinsically motivated efforts to achieve common objectives which may not be identified in advance (De Pree 1989). Given the strong ties that bind the covenantal partners, the relationship is not easily stretched to a breaking point, or threatened by disagreement or conflict (Van Dyne et al. 1994).

De Pree (1989) contrasted the notion of contractual and covenantal relationships. Contractual relationships are built on the basis of expectations, objectives, compensation, working conditions, benefits, timetables, or constraints. In contrast, covenantal relationships rest on the mutual intimacy among people and shared commitment to values, ideas, and goals, which enable work to be meaningful and fulfilling. While contractual relationships are necessary in organizations, they are insufficient to attract and retain the best people in organizations. As such, the best individuals work like volunteers who will be motivated by intangible things found in covenantal relationships.

As a form of relational contract, covenantal relationships shape the nature and quality of the employment relationship between employees and their employers,

© Springer International Publishing Switzerland 2015
S. Sendjaya, *Personal and Organizational Excellence through Servant Leadership*,
Management for Professionals, DOI 10.1007/978-3-319-16196-9_5

which in turn affect employee attitudes and behaviors (Morrison and Robinson 1997). Covenantal relationships are similar to other relational contracts such as psychological contracts and social exchange in that they are subjective, unwritten, and based on perceptions of reciprocal relationships (Graham and Organ 1993). However, unlike psychological contracts, covenantal relationships have a normative and moral component (Barnett and Schubert 2002) and entails acceptance and internationalization of organizational values (Van Dyne et al. 1994).

In covenantal relationships, employees feel valued and supported by the organization, which creates positive attitudes toward the organization and leads to desirable outcomes, such as obedience, loyalty, and participation (Graham and Organ 1993). Empirical research has shown that employee perceptions of covenantal relationships are positively associated with organizational citizenship behaviors (Van Dyne et al. 1994). In addition, covenantal relationships are positively linked with ethical work climates characterized by benevolence (social responsibility) and principle (adherence to law and professional codes), and negatively linked with work climates marked by egoism and economic efficiency (Barnett and Schubert 2002). In my theorizing of servant leadership, *Covenantal Relationship* was defined as behaviors of the leader that foster genuine, profound, and lasting relationships with followers. In order to build covenantal relationships with others, servant leaders rely on the following building blocks, namely acceptance, availability, equality, and collaboration.

5.1 Acceptance

Unlike most leaders who protect status symbols as a means of establishing distance between themselves and their followers, servant leaders accept others for who they are, not for how they make servant leaders feel. Some followers they work with have personality types and temperaments that are squarely opposite to those of their leaders. Leaders with unrealistic expectations about them will tend to personalize what is not personal, be offended, and respond in an adversarial manner. Servant leaders on the other hand deal with these differences gracefully, learning to appreciate, celebrate, and learn from these individually unique approaches, preferences, and styles. The ability of servant leaders to engage others with unqualified acceptance enables other people to experiment, grow, and be creative without fear (Daft and Lengel 2000). Bennis and Nanus (1985, p. 66) asserted that when leaders "'enter the skin' of someone else, to understand what other people are like on their terms, rather than judging them" is a sign of the leader's emotional wisdom. The strong ties that bind covenantal partners produce a solid and profound relationship that is not easily ruptured by either interpersonal or task conflicts.

The second form of servant leaders' acceptance concern their followers' past failures and wrongdoings. They realize that even the most talented followers are infallible. They are not immune from costly mistakes. They might say something grossly inappropriate to the leader. But servant leaders forgive and forget, then accepting them unconditionally and without judgment (Autry 2001). It does not mean that they act as if the wrong that their followers did become right. It means they do not carry a record of their followers' wrongs, then treating their followers in light of those wrongs. They simply refuse to be controlled by a bitter or judgmental heart, and put the leader-follower relationship at risk. Greenleaf (1977, p. 21) argued that this kind of acceptance requires a willingness to tolerate imperfection, as "anybody could lead perfect people – if they were any. But there aren't any perfect people." Hence, servant leaders accept others not by selecting perfect people, but by seeing imperfect people perfectly.

While servant leaders accept others unconditionally, they are not content with the status quo. Instead, servant leaders lift people up and encourage others to grow as persons and to be what they are capable of becoming (Greenleaf 1977).

5.2 Availability

Good leaders provide followers access to the resources they need to excel at work. This may include pertinent information, performance feedback, financial backup, expert view, and so on. Because servant leaders have a strong sense of secure self, they are willing to share the resources that would empower followers. More importantly than making these resources available, however, servant leaders make themselves available for others to build a genuine leader-follower relationship and nurture a culture of professional intimacy in the workplace such that there is no superficiality in relating with other people (De Pree 1992).

Frost (2003) asserted that in their interactions with followers, leaders become recipients of a wide range of emotions, which can be emotionally positive (e.g. respect and admiration) and negative (e.g. anger, fear, and distrust). Dealing with emotional pain in organizations that leaders encounter or create before they become toxic is a hidden work of leadership which necessitates professional intimacy between leaders and followers. The willingness of leaders to make themselves available in order to establish and cultivate intimate connections with others is indicative of their healthy functioning (Kets De Vries 2001).

More specifically, a tangible expression of a leader's availability can be found in the discipline of responding to any problem by listening first. Greenleaf (1977) maintained that servant leaders possess a natural tendency to engage with others by listening with intent to understand, as opposed to merely pretending to listen or selective listening. Genuine listening develops strength in other people and transforms the relationship between the leader and the led (Covey 1991). Kim and Mauborgne (1992, p. 124) in their observation of a Chinese parable posited that leaders need to learn the art of listening to both the spoken and unspoken words of others:

> For only when a ruler has learned to listen closely to the people's hearts, hearing their feelings uncommunicated, pains unexpressed, and complaints not spoken of, can he hope to inspire confidence in his people, understand something is wrong, and meet the true needs of

his citizens. The demise of states comes when leaders listen only to superficial words and do not penetrate deeply into the souls of the people to hear their true opinions, feelings, and desires.

One of the executives I interviewed echoed the same sentiment, highlighting the need to listen to the marginalized voices in the organization:

> I think quite often in the traditional system or structure, a leader is the one who dictates what's to be done. And certainly that's my background. In the old days, I thought my role is to tell people what to do. But in my current role I learn that quite often it's the little voices that matter. We are meant to listen to become better leaders.

5.3   Equality

The notion of equality or equity is closely associated with perceptions of fairness (Deluga 1994), the absence of which would trigger a behavioral reaction on the part of followers to eliminate perceptions of inequity by intentionally minimizing their contributions. Equality is a key leadership trust-building activity which has been positively correlated with followers' organizational citizenship behaviors (Deluga 1994). In the organizational context, the perceived fairness of treatment from an organization is typically researched under the term organizational justice comprising distributed, procedural, and interactional justice (Aryee et al. 2002).

Patterson (2004) noted that servant leaders treat all people with radical equality, engaging with others as equal partners in the organization. They do not establish or maintain a vertical distance with their followers to bolster their legitimate authority or status symbols. On the other hand, servant leaders seek to bridge the distance between themselves and other individuals so that they can be part of the group (Marshall 1991). De Pree (1992, p. 27) asserted that equity is the distinctive domain of a leader, in the sense that leaders ought to give everyone "the chance to advance in the organization and the chance to reach one's potential." At TDIndustries, a Texas-based national mechanical construction and service firm that has been consistently ranked as one of the best employers in the US, its 1,300-plus employees are known and treated as 'Partners' in every sense of the word (Spears and Lawrence 2002). Collectively they own 94 % of the company shares, the remaining 6 % is owned by its second-generation founder and CEO Jack Lowe, Jr. Regardless of their organizational rank, each partner and their families receive excellent health care package with an average of 70 % of its coverage paid for by the company. This radical way to treat employees is attributed by Lowe to the philosophy of servant leadership.

Servant leaders do not only treat employees equally, but they also pay a specific attention to the weakest members of the organization. The acid test of servant leadership is whether the least privileged individuals in any group, organization, or society show positive signs of improvement emotionally, psychologically, and financially. Since a chain is only as strong as its weakest link and organizations can go as fast as their slowest members, servant leaders ensure that those who are the least presentable get an equal access and opportunity as others.

The following interview comment from a CEO shows that the equality that servant leaders seek to model sometimes becomes quite a personal matter. His decision however speaks volume about servant leadership in action.

> We succeed or fail together. Because you're packing boxes does not mean that you're a lonely being that should be shunned. Actually what that person does has an impact on the success of the business. And what they do is valuable. It really is. If they didn't do that, a part of the business would struggle to make money. This is embodied in the organization in some of the things that we do. I have arguments with my board about their wanting to pay me more money because I don't want a big discrepancy between my salary and other people's salary. I think pay levels awarded to some CEOs are completely absurd. There is no justification for it . . . It doesn't make any sense. Okay, fine, it needs to be at least at a minimum level, because this is published externally. But I literally argued just to keep it down. Because I don't want to be seen to be separating myself out from the rest of the group that I am trying to lead.

5.4 Collaboration

The highly uncertain and volatile business environment requires a new set of skills and talents, greater than any single individual is likely to possess. This daunting reality has become the impetus for the emergence of collaborative leadership (Gronn 1999). Numerous terms in the literature refer to the notion of collaborative leadership, namely democratic leadership (Bass 1990), distributed leadership (Barry 1991; Gronn 1999), and collective leadership (Burns 1998). Collaborative leadership is often contrasted with dictatorial leadership as they represent the two extremes along the continuum of leadership practices (Bass 1990).

Barry (1991, p. 34) defined collaborative leadership as "a collection of roles and behaviors that can be split apart, shared, rotated, and used sequentially or concomitantly", which suggests that multiple leaders can exist in a team or an organization simultaneously, with each leader assuming a different but complementary role. This leadership approach fosters the active cultivation and development of leadership abilities within all team or organizational members (Barry 1991). Implicitly assumed in the argument is the possession of certain leadership qualities by individuals other than the leader to be exercised at some point. Burns (1978) has long recognized leadership as a distributed process carried out by many members of an organization or society. It brings about changes at the macro level (organizations or societies) as well as the individual level. Implied in this conceptualization of collective leadership is the notion that leadership functions are shared at all levels in the organization based on the task to be performed and the skills required to perform it. More recently, Burns (1998) restated this view by asserting that leadership should not be understood simply as a narrow dichotomy between leaders and followers. Instead, it must be viewed as a dynamic interplay among different organizational members. The dynamic, collective interrelationships among the organizational members provide a new perspective on the commonly held notion about leadership and the leader. Servant leaders builds such relationship by expecting people to collaborate and creating a positive culture of collaboration to create a synergy. The following interview comment illustrates how a servant leader views collaboration in the work context:

> In a servant leadership situation, there's more understanding of everyone's contribution towards an end goal and undoubtedly in my view you get more loyalty from your people, more commitment from your people to that particular strategy or goal or decision. And when people work together to achieve something as opposed to one person trying to work achieve it, it makes a huge difference in the process. I definitely think that there is a tremendous synergy in a servant leadership approach as opposed to a more I'm-the-boss-and-I'm-making-all-the-decision style.

However, Kofman and Senge (1993) argued that collaboration is often difficult given our preoccupation with competition. While competition in itself is not necessarily bad, and at times is required for organizational survival or success, the tendency to overemphasize it has prevented leaders to search for avenues of collaboration: "Fascinated with competition, we often find ourselves competing with the very people with whom we need to collaborate . . . Our overemphasis on competition makes *looking* good more important than *being* good" (Kofman and Senge 1993, p. 9).

Bennis and Biederman (1997) argued that when leaders bring together people from a variety of backgrounds and disciplines, the group gets better results through the collective support and fellowship needed for sustaining its performance. Leaders who nurture cooperative relationships can inspire commitment and are perceived to competent, whereas competitive and independent leaders are perceived to be obstructive and ineffective (Tjosvold and Tjosvold 1991). Servant leaders always foster collaboration with others, much like jazz-band leaders who capitalize on the unique talents of people (De Pree 1992, p. 103):

> A leader will pick up the tune, set the tempo, and start the music, define a "style." After that, it's up to the band to be disciplined and free, wild and restrained – leaders and followers, focused and wide-ranging, playing the music for the audience and accountable to the requirements of the band. Jazz-band leaders know how to integrate the "voices" in the band without diminishing their uniqueness. The individuals in the band are expected to play solo and together. What a wonderful way to think of a vital and productive organization.

5.5   Actionable Commitments of Servant Leadership

The following actionable commitments are taken from the above four of *Covenantal Relationship* dimension. As they are derived from reliable and valid measure of servant leadership behavior, they can be used with confidence for personal reflection or group discussion in different settings and cultures.

Commitment #14 – Affirm my trust in others
Negativity in the workplace is rampant and contagious, crippling employees' morale and making them feel undervalued. Try to swim upstream against this current. Affirm others' strengths, abilities, and gifts. Be on the lookout for something

positive that you see in action to compliment, the more specific the better the ripple effect would be. Remind everyone in the organizational hierarchy their equal importance to the organization.

Commitment #15 – Accept others as they are, irrespective of their failures

People do make mistakes, and that includes you. The sooner you can accept that, the less likely you will dwell in the past and see them in the shadow of their past records. Accepts them for who they are, not as you want them to be. Otherwise, it'd be you, not they, who would still be imprisoned in the past. Forgive, forget, and foresee what they could become in the future because of the lessons learned from their mistakes.

Commitment #16 – Respect others for who they are, not how they make me feel

First of all, you are not the center of the universe. And your true self should not comprise of the net effect of what other people do to you. Finally, if you spend an enormous amount of energy making up your minds about each individual, your leadership will feel like running a marathon while carrying a huge backpack. Those idiosyncratic attitudes and habits that people show should not dictate your respect to them. You respect them because they are created equal.

Commitment #17 – Treat people as equal partners

This one goes beyond the common decency of treating everyone as equals with no favoritism. Politically correct leaders are just that. What matters more is the internal terrain of your heart attitudes towards others who are different than you in all sorts of ways. See if your spontaneous thoughts, uncensored words, and knee-jerk reactions towards them reveal how you really see them.

Commitment #18 – Spend time to build a professional relationship with others

The time you spend together with your individual staff should not only be performance-based. Get interested in their lives outside work. When they realize you have no hidden agendas, your genuine, nonjudgmental presence turns you into a safe place for people to be vulnerable at.

Commitment #19 – Have confidence in others, even when the risk seems great

Here is the difference between belief and trust. To believe is to have confidence that the man who walks a tightrope stretched across the Niagara Falls would make it. To trust is to be willing to hop on his back with him on the return tightrope-walk. Trusting others is a risky business but brings you high return on investment.

References

Aryee, S., Budhwar, P. S., & Chen, Z. X. (2002). Trust as a mediator of the relationship between organizational justice and work outcomes: Test of a social exchange model. *Journal of Organizational Behavior, 23,* 267–285.

Autry, J. A. (2001). *The servant leader*. Roseville: Prima.

Barnett, T., & Schubert, E. (2002). Perceptions of the ethical work climate and covenantal relationship. *Journal of Business Ethics, 36*(3), 279–290.

Barry, D. (1991). Managing the bossless team: Lessons in distributed leadership. *Organizational Dynamics, 20*(1), 31–47.

Bass, B. M. (1990). *Bass and Stogdill's handbook of leadership* (3rd ed.). New York: The Free Press.

Bennis, W. G., & Biederman, P. W. (1997). *Organizing genius: The secrets of creative collaboration*. Reading: Addison-Wesley.

Bennis, W. G., & Nanus, B. (1985). *Leaders: The strategies for taking charge*. New York: Harper & Row.

Bromley, D. G., & Busching, B. C. (1988). Understanding the structure of contractual and covenantal social relations: Implications for the sociology of religion. *Sociological Analysis, 49*, 15–32.

Burns, J. M. (1978). *Leadership*. New York: Harper & Row.

Burns, J. M. (1998). Empowerment for change. In *Rethinking leadership working papers*. College Park: Academy of Leadership Press.

Covey, S. R. (1991). *Principle-centered leadership*. New York: Fireside.

Daft, R. L., & Lengel, R. H. (2000). *Fusion leadership: Unlocking the subtle forces that change people and organizations*. San Francisco: Berrett-Koehler.

De Pree, M. (1989). *Leadership is an art*. New York: Dell Publishing.

Deluga, R. J. (1994). Supervisor trust building, leader-member exchange and organizational citizenship behaviour. *Journal of Occupational and Organizational Psychology, 67*, 315–326.

DePree, M. (1992). *Leadership Jazz*. New York: Currency Doubleday.

Elazar, D. J. (1980). The political theory of covenant: Biblical origin and modern development. *Publius, 10*(4), 3–30.

Frost, P. J. (2003). *Toxic emotions at work: How compassionate managers handle pain and conflict*. Boston: Harvard Business School Publications.

Graham, J. W., & Organ, D. W. (1993). Commitment and covenantal organization. *Journal of Managerial Issues, 5*(4), 483–502.

Greenleaf, R. K. (1977). *Servant leadership*. Mahwah: Paulist Press.

Gronn, P. (1999). *Systems of distributed leadership in organizations*. Paper presented at the Annual meeting of the American Educational Research Association, Montreal, Canada.

Kets De Vries, M. F. R. (2001). Creating authentizotic organizations: Well-functioning individuals in vibrant companies. *Human Relations, 54*(1), 101–111.

Kim, W. C., & Mauborgne, R. A. (1992). Parables of leadership. *Harvard Business Review, 70*(4), 123–129.

Kofman, F., & Senge, P. M. (1993). Communities of commitment: The heart of learning organization. *Organizational Dynamics, 22*(2), 5–24.

Marshall, T. (1991). *Understanding leadership: Fresh perspectives on the essentials of New Testament leadership*. Chichester: Sovereign World.

Morrison, E. W., & Robinson, S. L. (1997). When employees feel betrayed: A model of how psychological contract violation develops. *Academy of Management Review, 22*, 226–256.

Patterson, K. (2004). *Servant leadership: A theoretical model*. Paper presented at the Servant Leadership Research Roundtable, Virginia Beach, VA.

Spears, L. C., & Lawrence, M. (2002). *Focus on leadership: Servant-leadership for the twenty-first century*. New York: Wiley.

Tjosvold, D. W., & Tjosvold, M. M. (1991). *Leading the team organization: How to create an enduring competitive advantage*. New York: Lexington Books.

Van Dyne, L., Graham, J. W., & Dienesch, R. M. (1994). Organizational citizenship behavior: Construct redefinition, measurement, and validation. *Academy of Management Journal, 37*(4), 765–792.

Responsible Morality

6

Morality is not the doctrine of how we may make ourselves happy, but how we make ourselves worthy of our happiness.
(Immanuel Kant)

Cases of blatantly corrupt leadership and their disastrous outcomes in contemporary organizations era remain ubiquitous. Against such backdrop, the importance of leadership practices that foster ethical decisions and actions cannot be overstated. As far as leaders are concerned, being highly capable to deliver bottom line results is not only insufficient but often becomes a fertile ground to grow seeds of moral compromises. Granted effective but unethical leadership may take individuals and organizations to the top, but by design such leadership will destroy both from inside like a spreading cancer. The difference between leadership that is built to last from one that is built to flip is a balance between being effective and ethical. In the words of Ciulla (1995), superior leadership entails both technical competencies and moral capacities. In fact, the morality dimension of leadership is vital in a leader-follower relationship, since the exercise of authority and power always entails ethical challenges (Hollander 1995).

Researchers concur that ethical leadership is a key dimension of effective organizations, and highlight the urgency for leaders to reflect on their moral judgment and foster moral action (Trevino and Brown 2004). Unfortunately amidst morally flawed corporate leaders, the need for "moral, uplifting, transcending leadership" (Burns 1978, p. 452) typically becomes a nice rhetoric that always gets neglected. While various reasons have been offered to explain why it rarely goes beyond an insightful discussion in the boardroom or university lecture halls, they boil down to the increasingly popular view that *moral leadership* is a contradiction in terms.

© Springer International Publishing Switzerland 2015
S. Sendjaya, *Personal and Organizational Excellence through Servant Leadership*,
Management for Professionals, DOI 10.1007/978-3-319-16196-9_6

6.1   Is Moral Leadership an Oxymoron?

Researchers such as Rost (1993, 1995) rejects morality as a leadership requirement on the ground that it is impossible for everyone to agree as to what is a high moral standard. Different worldviews and beliefs that people hold make a common understanding of what constitutes morality unattainable. He further argues that in the presence of his understanding of ethical pluralism and moral relativism across different individuals or cultures, it is inappropriate for ethics or morality to be attached to leadership. In short, the subjectivity of each individual's beliefs makes moral value a limiting factor in the understanding of leadership.

Complementing such view is the shift of understanding on the virtue of tolerance. Carson (2012) noted that tolerance used to be typically defined in any dictionary somewhere along the line of 'acceptance of existence of different views' (e.g., in political, religious, moral spheres). Implied within this definition are two visible attitudes, namely respecting other views or beliefs or practices without necessarily agreeing, sympathizing, or supporting, and recognizing that proponents of those differing views, beliefs, or practices have every right to hold or defend them. However there has been a radical shift of understanding in the last century from 'acceptance of existence of different views' to 'acceptance of different views.' While this shift may sound subtle in form, it is massive in substance in that the new meaning necessitates its subscribers to accept an opposing view to be equally as their own. To beg to differ according to this new meaning is therefore intolerant, as Carson (2012, p. 12) points out:

> Intolerance is no longer a refusal to allow contrary opinions to say their piece in public, but must be understood to be any questioning or contradicting the view that all opinions are equal in value, that all worldviews have equal worth, that all stances are equally valid. To question such postmodern axioms is by definition intolerant.

In other words, to be tolerant under the old understanding means "I disagree with your views because they are wrong, but I respect them and you have the right to hold and defend them" whereas today it means "I cannot judge whether your views are right or wrong because everyone is equally right and wrong. Nobody is more right than anyone. Otherwise I am being intolerant". This incoherent tautology becomes a classic catch-22 when those who are not willing to accept this new meaning of tolerance are therefore considered extremely intolerant.

The following questions are helpful to think through the application of the above abstraction on leadership. Is Hitler a noble leader or horrible tyrant? Is bin Laden a terrorist or freedom fighter? According to the postmodern view of leadership, it is futile to answer such questions given our moral and cultural relativism. Further, to choose one option over the other is considered intolerant. Rather than articulating our beliefs and refuting those we disagree with while respecting those on the opposite side, we should instead assert that all claims are equally valid. As tolerance becomes embedded deep within the plausibility structure of our society, every judgment, therefore, is all a matter of personal opinion because everything is relative.

At the heart of this epistemological discrepancy is a basic underlying assumption whether objective morality exists. In the absence of objective morality one can make any claims about moral judgments according to his or her subjective moral taste, and no one has the right to refute it or running the risk of being labeled intolerant. To say that morality is the *sine qua non* of leadership is therefore meaningless because there are no common frameworks for resolving moral disputes or for reaching agreement on ethical matters.

However, believing in subjective morality and applying it to leadership is problematic. To believe that morality is subjective essentially means that each of us is free, morally speaking, to choose whichever moral point of view we find most appealing and worthwhile. In the context of leadership, this would mean that the choice of becoming Mother Teresa or Saddam Hussein would be roughly the same as it were to become a football player or a basketball player. If morality is entirely subjective, it follows that Hitler's holocaust is not really wrong in any objective sense that is morally binding on others. At best, such atrocity simply offends our personal moral taste or violates our preconceived worldview of morality. In other words, if we choose to dislike it is simply because we find it unappealing. But we can never pass judgment that it is wrong, let alone condemn it. On the contrary, if we believe that there is a crucial moral difference between the leadership approach of Hitler and that of Gandhi, it follows that not all moral judgments or values are equally right.

Relativism as a moral theory is arbitrary and unfounded because its proponents merely assume but can never prove it is true. It refutes itself when it rejects the absolute laws of rationality and logic. Those who claim "There are no absolute truths" or "Everything is relative" engage in self-refuting exercise as these statements are grammatically sound but logically flawed. It fails to see the unspoken assumption behind the very dogmatic statements they supposedly reject – "There are no absolutes (except this one)" or "(I am certain that) everything is relative." A leader who advises his followers, "Trust no one!" contradicts himself because in the course of doing so, he is in fact inviting them to trust him. Simply put, relativism promotes what it denies. The more adamant the relativistic leader argues (e.g., "You need to absolutely trust me 100 % on this", "trust no one!"), the more absurd and incoherent he would be.

On the contrary, the existence of objective moral values can be demonstrated by the deontological pattern of moral reasoning which requires one to perform actions which are intrinsically right, that is as a sense of moral obligation. In his seminal work *Groundwork of the Metaphysic of Morals,* Kant (1964, p. 70) outlined the principle of universality as follows: "Act as if the maxim of thy action were to become by thy will a universal law of nature", implying that one ought to act in such a way that the principle according to which the action is performed can be accepted as a universal law of morality. In other words, an act is morally right if one is willing to universalize the rule of action which generates that particular act (Guyer 2002). Sergiovanni (1992, p. 20), who based his concept of moral leadership upon deontological ethics, echoed Kant's argument that any acts are justified as moral acts only if they are done "in the belief and because of the belief that it is right – from duty, not because of personal inclination, gain, or love." Even enlightened management techniques or leadership methods which are seemingly empowering would not be morally worthy if they were undertaken solely to increase the shareholder value, and not out of a sense of duty (Bowie 2000).

Building on the first principle, Kant (1964, pp. 75–76) proposed the principle of humanity which provides an even stronger basis for moral leadership: "Act in such a way that you always treat humanity, whether in your own person or in the person of any other, never simply as a means, but always at the same time as an end." This formulation implies that other people is not merely a stepping stone for a leader's own personal fulfillment. Instead they are legitimate ends in and of themselves, and are valuable for their own sakes. Therefore, leaders must always treat their followers never as a means toward advancing the leader's own preconceived needs. Bowie (2000) asserted that the extent to which leaders respect and foster the autonomy of their followers characterizes a Kantian perspective of leadership. Deontological ethics therefore stands in contrast to the popular adage 'The end justifies the means' rooted in a Machiavellian code of morality. The means and the ends are of the same importance and both must be ethical. Every act born out of the desire for pleasure, power and respect from others is deemed by Kant to be morally worthless. Hence, Sergiovanni (1992) describes moral leadership as a new kind of leadership practice that is rooted in moral authority.

Graham (1991) argued that servant leadership is distinct from other leadership approaches because of its emphasis on followers' development, specifically in the area of responsible morality. Specifically, servant leaders elevate both leaders' and employees' moral convictions and actions. This dimension of servant leadership is manifested in the leader's moral reasoning and moral action. Because servant leaders are morally principled leaders, one can expect to observe in them a pattern of alignment between their words and deeds, between their espoused principles or values and actual actions. They walk their talks and talk their walks.

6.2 Moral Reasoning

Moral reasoning refers to the implicit cognitive processing used to justify one's decisions or actions (Kohlberg 1984). It does not necessarily gauge the strength of one's actual moral position. Instead it signals the level at which one is capable of cognitively reasoning while maintaining a moral point of view. It concerns the real motive behind one's chosen course of action by processing their implicit morality. Thus moral reasoning empowers individuals to make sense of and integrate moral values, thereby improving their capacity to undertake moral decisions and actions (Kohlberg 1969; Piaget and Gabain 1966).

On the basis of his observations of moral development stages of children growing up to adulthood, Kohlberg (1981, 1984) proposed a moral reasoning theory comprising three levels of cognitive moral development (Rest 1994): Pre-conventional, conventional and post-conventional. Individuals operating within the *pre-conventional* level are characterized by an egocentric motive to avoid punishment and seek reward. Those operating within the *conventional* level are driven by strong conformity to social expectations and compliance to rules to decide right or wrong. Finally, individuals operating within the *post-conventional* level rely on internalized universal values which transcend social expectations to guide their actions. Post-conventional moral individuals may criticize and behave against rules or laws that do not serve a universal principle such as human dignity or justice. The key point of Kohlberg's (1969) theories is that one's moral decisions and actions are determined by one's level of moral reasoning.

Based on this theory, an executive might decide to mentor a junior recruit from a minority group in his organization because of the ensuing positive image he would be able to project to his superiors as an inclusive leader which would advance his career (pre-conventional motive), or for the sake of conforming to the politically correct expectation of the CEO (conventional motive), or because it is the right thing to do given that everyone is born equal (post-conventional motive). Granted these motives are quite distinct, but few leaders take the time to stop and reflect on why they do what they do. Often the type of a priori moral inquiry is superficially done on the run by engaging in simple questions like "If I make that decision, would I be able to sleep well tonight?" or "Would I feel embarrassed if my face appears on the front page of the morning newspaper following the decision I am about to make?" In the name of speed and efficiency, often a more sophisticated moral reflection is glaringly absent. Badaracco (1998, p. 116) asserts that "the most satisfied business leaders are the ones who are able to dig below the busy surface of their daily lives and refocus on their core values and principles."

Graham (1995) argued that servant leadership models and promotes moral reasoning, fully aware that it is indispensable for the leader's own moral safeguard as every leader particularly successful leaders are prone to the danger of putting themselves beyond the scope of moral requirements which apply to everyone (Price 2000). Specifically servant leaders enhance the capacity for moral reasoning by engaging with others in leader-follower moral dialogue, probing each other back and forth to evaluate the impact of their options, considering the concerns and interests of others, and challenge their respective moral motives. Graham (1991) also argued that servant leadership employs relational power which facilitates intense yet respectful moral dialogue between leaders and followers, a practice considered challenging by other forms of leadership that rely on hierarchical power. Since dialogue enables each participant to suspend assumption and engage in genuine conversation which, in turn, leads to new insights (Senge 1990), it can also be useful for bringing into light ethical assumptions, patterns of interactions, policies, and practices counterproductive to the organization and its members (Gottlieb and Jyotsna 1996). In doing so, servant leaders examine the ethics not only of the followers or the organization, but also of the leaders themselves.

The ultimate goal of moral reasoning that servant leaders engage followers in is to move them forward to the post-conventional moral reasoning level. Leaders with post-conventional moral reasoning tend to assume a teaching role in a group (Dukerich et al. 1990) and in turn followers with post-conventional moral reasoning are more likely to become champions in building the ethical climate of the organization and engaging others to uphold the ethical thought processes undergirding an organization's climate (Lewin and Stephen 1994; Trevino et al. 2000). In an organizational context where ethical principles are typically compromised, servant leadership fosters reflective behaviors which bring about positive changes in the ethical climate of the organization.

6.3   Moral Action

Jackall (1988) observed that organizational bureaucracy plays an important role in shaping the moral consciousness of managers. In order to survive in the corporate culture, managers are often compelled to morally compromise, and conform to the belief that "what is right in the corporation is what the guy above you wants from you" (Jackall 1988, p. 6). In view of this organizational reality, servant leadership has been considered more likely than transformational and transactional leadership to foster reflective behavior. Responsible reflection allows organizational members to respect and value differing interests of the various organizational stakeholders (Giampetro-Meyer et al. 1998; Graham 1995), and therefore are more likely to engage in moral actions.

Moral action is a behavioral manifestation, verbal or non-verbal, that one undertakes on the basis of moral deliberation. The difference between moral reasoning and moral action is analogous to the difference between implicit theory and theory-in-use. Researchers generally concur that moral action is significantly associated with moral reasoning (Blasi 1980; Thoma and Rest 1986). Leaders with a mature level of moral reasoning tend to value goals and engage in actions which do not serve their own interests, but those of others (Turner et al. 2002), an inclination which is consonant with servant leadership. The close association of moral action and leadership is well documented in the literature. As early as in 1938 Chester Barnard (1938) in his seminal work *The Functions of the Executive* argued that a distinguishing hallmark of executive work is developing organizational morals and codes of ethics.

Leaders play a pivotal role in building, maintaining, and changing the corporate culture (Schein 1992, 1996, 1999), which in turn affects the ethical behavior of all organizational members (Reidenbach and Robin 1991; Sims 1992). More importantly, the behaviors of leaders define the ethical framework of the organization via social influence processes which govern the behaviors of employees (Weiss 1977). According to Schein (1999, p. 98), what leaders "pay attention to, measure, get upset about, reward, and punish" in everyday routines are far more vital than what they espouse, publish, or preach. The ways leaders affect ethical culture have less to do with charisma and more to do with serving as a living example of core values that make up the culture (Kotter and Heskett 1992).

Schein (1999) proposed primary and secondary culture-building mechanisms in relation to building and shaping culture. On the basis of the primary culture-building mechanisms, servant leaders can evaluate to what extent they foster an ethical culture in their organizations (Table 6.1).

Table 6.1 Primary and secondary culture-building mechanisms

Culture-building mechanisms	Relevant questions
What leaders pay attention to, measure, and control on a regular basis	How do people gain power in the organization? Does promotion criteria include evidence of ethical leadership?
How leaders react to critical incidents and organizational crises	To what extent ethical values are upheld or compromised during crises? How does one stay out of trouble?
Observed criteria by which leaders allocate scarce resources	To what extent organizational resources allocated to star performers who ignore ethical guidelines?
Deliberate role modeling, teaching, and coaching	Do the leaders walk the talk ethically? Do they talk about the important of ethics repeatedly through different means?
Observed criteria by which leaders allocate rewards and status	Is there any unwritten rule to get ahead? Do people who behave ethically get recognized and rewarded?
Observed criteria by which leaders recruit, select, promote, retire, and excommunicate organizational members	Is recruitment focused merely on past achievements as well as evidence of moral integrity and courage? Are there clear and consistent consequences of unethical conduct?

Bass and Steidlmeier (1999) maintained that there are three components of moral action, namely the ends sought, the means employed, and the consequences, which can serve as a guide to differentiate right from wrong. As transforming leaders and servant leaders always appeal to higher ideals, moral values, and the higher-order needs of followers (Yukl 1990), they are more likely to ensure that both the ends they seek and the means they employ can be morally legitimized, thoughtfully reasoned and ethically justified (Sendjaya 2005). Accordingly, genuine leadership takes place only when leaders' and followers' ethical aspirations are enhanced as a result of their interactions.

In summary, the moral reasoning that servant leaders employ and moral action they model will contribute to followers' moral identity, which in turn, will guide their ethical decisions and actions. The capacity for engaging others in moral dialogue is useful not only to examine the ethics of the followers, but also that of the organization, as well as of the leaders themselves. Servant leadership therefore is likely to build the 'socio-moral' climate of the organization (Wyld and Jones 1997) or the ethical norms characterizing a social setting which in turn will affect the moral decision-making and behavior of the individuals within it (Sims 1992).

6.4   Servant vs Machiavellian Leader

Given Blasi's (1980) theorizing that consistency between moral judgment and behavior could also depend upon the relative strength of several simultaneous and conflicting behavioral tendencies such as competition, self-protection, and self-promotion, Machiavellianism can moderate the relationship between moral reasoning and moral action (Sendjaya et al. 2014). Servant leaders therefore are not naïve, they are fully aware that even leaders with sophisticated moral reasoning may still have seeds of self-serving tendencies within them (e.g., 'I need to look out for me, otherwise who will?', 'Why would I risk my career by helping someone?'). The probability of acting on one's moral reasoning capacity can easily be affected by a Machiavellian value orientation.

Dahling et al. (2009, p. 219) defines Machiavellianism as "one's propensity to distrust others, engage in amoral manipulation, seek control over others, and seek status for oneself." While it includes an observable dimension (i.e., amoral manipulation), those who are highly Machiavellians do not constantly and actively engage in amoral manipulation. They are ready to flex their moral muscle, and may engage in pro-organizational behaviors in a friendly manner or deviant behaviors in a subtle manner, whichever serve their goals and interests better. As such, Machiavellianism is an individual difference variable that functions as an instrumental value: that the end justifies the means.

Machiavellian leaders can behave in a chameleon manner, changing their shape at will to suit their surrounding out of self-preservation or self-profit motives. While the notion of chameleon affect may refer to something neutral such as nonconscious behavioral mimicry (Chartrand and Bargh 1999), it often has a more negative trajectory. In their study, Sherry et al. (2006) found that Machiavellianism correlates positively with perfectionistic self-presentation, that is Machiavellians will project an image of superiority and perfection to others. As such, we contend that this chameleon-like repertoire may propel them to appear servant-like for the sake of expediency. This shape-shifting capacity is in keeping with their dominant, mistrustful, and exploitative tendency.

The second possible route is less overt. As every 2-year old will inevitable demonstrates, there is a Machiavellian streak in every human being. While this individual difference gets suppressed through positive nurture, education, and training, it simply lays dormant like a sleeper cell but can be activated with the right triggers. Hence, high Machiavellians might be groomed and trained to be authentic leaders, behave authentically, perceive themselves and are perceived by others as authentic leaders for years until such time when a personal or professional pressure brings that Machiavellian tendency to the fore.

The following table shows a contrast between a Machiavellian and Servant mindset, based on the 5-item amoral dimension of the Machiavellianism Personality Scale (MPS) developed by Dahling et al. (2009). While no one is utterly Machiavellian (or a perfect servant leader, for that matter), it is useful for leaders to reflect which trajectory they tend to show in their leadership (Table 6.2).

6.5   Actionable Commitments of Servant Leadership

The following commitments are identical to the ones on the right hand column on the above table, and relate to the dimension of *Responsible Morality*. They are expanded with short commentaries to maximize their practical usefulness. As with other commitments, they are part of the servant leadership behavior scale (SLBS).

Table 6.2 The contrast between Machiavellian leader vs Servant leader

Machiavellian leader	Servant leader
I am willing to be unethical if I believe it will help me succeed	I take a resolute stand on moral principles at all times
I am willing to sabotage the efforts of other people if they threaten my own goals	I would employ morally justified means to achieve legitimate ends
I would cheat if there was a low chance of getting caught	I do not believe in 'the end justifies the means'
I believe that lying is necessary to maintain a competitive advantage over others	I believe doing what is right is more important than looking good
The only good reason to talk to others is to get information that I can use to my benefits	When I talk to others, I often engage them in moral dialogue to enhance their capacity for moral actions

Commitment #20 – Take a resolute stand on moral principles at all times

It does not mean that you are unnecessarily dogmatic or annoyingly standoffish. Rather it speaks of insisting to put first things first. If you do not stand for a few moral principles, you will fall for any moral dilemma. Ensure others know what you will stand for, and what you will not.

Commitment #21 – Encourage others to engage in moral reasoning

Engage others to examine from moral-laden perspectives work-related controversial issues and ethical dilemma (e.g., employing child labors). Do not merely ping-pong answers or solutions back and forth, rather entertain the issue, suspend assumptions, probe with curiosity until a deeper understanding of the issue emerges because of that collective interchange. Use these sessions as teachable moments to help them grow in their moral reasoning capacity.

Commitment #22 – Enhance others' capacity for moral actions

Moral courage is caught rather than taught, thus setting a positive example in this area is key in empowering others to do the same. Be honest however about your moral *lack* of courage. Show them that being courageous does not mean being fearless, but it is about believing that there is something far more important than fear. Plan regular sessions where real case studies from your or other organizations are used as springboards to gauge their likely responses. A good way to end such sessions is to ask "What one thing that you would start doing, and stop doing, to embody the lesson learned today? How do you ensure you will follow that through?"

Commitment #23 – Employ morally justified means to achieve legitimate ends

Your character is not formed in five most significant moments you have in life, rather it is shaped by 10,000 minor compromises you make. Every time you say to yourself 'no one will ever know' or 'everyone else does it', or 'I deserve this', or worse of all, rationalizing with all three excuses, you are gradually turning into someone new. It takes wisdom to recognize this because we are hardwired to respond to dramatic events, not slowly developing threats to our moral character.

Scrutinize the means used and ends sought to come up with a morally responsible course of action.

Commitment #24 – Emphasize on doing what is right rather than looking good
If you main concern as a leader is to be popular, perhaps you should consider clown-ship instead of leadership. In fact, leaders are more like parenting than entertaining people. The deeper the parents love toward their children, the more they hate the potentially destructive things within the children and will do anything in their power to remove of minimize regardless of the protest. Granted followers are not children, but the principle remains. Many leadership casualties could have been averted had leaders cared less about losing face. Explain firmly and gently the long-term consequences of each route taken, and the rationale why you think the unpopular option must be taken.

References

Badaracco, J. L., Jr. (1998). The discipline of building character. *Harvard Business Review, 76*(2), 114–124.

Barnard, C. I. (1938). *The functions of the executive*. Cambridge, MA: Harvard University Press.

Bass, B. M., & Steidlmeier, P. (1999). Ethics, character, and authentic transformational leadership behavior. *The Leadership Quarterly, 10*(2), 181–217.

Blasi, A. (1980). Bridging moral cognition and moral action: A critical review of the literature. *Psychological Bulletin, 88*(1), 129–161.

Bowie, N. A. (2000). Kantian theory of leadership. *Leadership & Organization Development Journal, 21*(4), 185–193.

Burns, J. M. (1978). *Leadership*. New York: Harper & Row.

Carson, D. A. (2012). *The intolerance of tolerance*. Grand Rapids: Wm. B. Eerdmans.

Chartrand, T. L., & Bargh, J. A. (1999). The chameleon effect: The perception-behavior link and social interaction. *Journal of Personality and Social Psychology, 76*, 893–910.

Ciulla, J. B. (1995). Leadership ethics: Mapping the territory. *Business Ethics Quarterly, 5*(1), 5–25.

Dahling, J. J., Whitaker, B. G., & Levy, P. E. (2009). The development and validation of a new Machiavellianism scale. *Journal of Management, 35*, 219–257.

Dukerich, J. M., Nichols, M. L., Elm, D. R., & Vollrath, D. A. (1990). Moral reasonings in group: Leaders make a difference. *Human Relations, 43*, 473–493.

Giampetro-Meyer, A., Brown, T., Browne, M. N., & Kubasek, N. (1998). Do we really want more leaders in business? *Journal of Business Ethics, 17*(15), 1727–1736.

Gottlieb, J. Z., & Jyotsna, S. (1996). Towards an ethical dimension of decision making in organizations. *Journal of Business Ethics, 15*(12), 1275–1285.

Graham, J. (1991). Servant-leadership in organizations: Inspirational and moral. *The Leadership Quarterly, 2*(2), 105–119.

Graham, J. W. (1995). Leadership, moral development, and citizenship behavior. *Business Ethics Quarterly, 5*(1), 43–54.

Guyer, P. (2002). Ends of reason and ends of nature: The place of teleology in Kant's ethics. *The Journal of Value Inquiry, 36*, 161–186.

Hollander, E. P. (1995). Ethical challenges in the leader-follower relationship. *Business Ethics Quarterly, 5*(1), 55–65.

Jackall, R. (1988). *Moral mazes: The world of corporate managers*. New York: Oxford University.

Kant, I. (1964). *Groundwork of the metaphysics of morals* (H. J. Paton, Trans.). New York: Harper.

Kohlberg, L. (1981). *The philosophy of moral development: Moral stages and the idea of justice* (Essays on moral development, Vol. 1). San Francisco: Harper & Row.

Kohlberg, L. (1984). *The psychology of moral development: The nature and validity of moral stages*. San Francisco: Harper & Row.

Kohlberg, L. (1969). *Stages in the development of moral thought and action.* New York: Holt, Rinehart, & Winston.

Kotter, J. P., & Heskett, J. L. (1992). *Corporate culture and performance.* New York: Free Press.

Lewin, A. Y., & Stephen, C. U. (1994). CEO attitudes as determinants of organization design: An integrated model. *Organization Studies, 15*(2), 183–212.

Piaget, J., & Gabain, M. (1966). *The moral judgment of the child.* New York: Free Press.

Price, T. L. (2000). Explaining ethical failures of leadership. *Leadership & Organization Development Journal, 21*(4), 177–184.

Reidenbach, R. E., & Robin, D. P. (1991). A conceptual model of corporate model development. *Journal of Business Ethics, 19,* 273–284.

Rest, J. R. (1994). Background: Theory and research. In J. R. Rest & D. Narvaez (Eds.), *Moral development in the professions* (pp. 1–26). Hillsdale: Erlbaum.

Rost, J. C. (1993). *Leadership for the twenty-first century.* Westport: Praeger.

Rost, J. C. (1995). Leadership: A discussion about ethics. *Business Ethics Quarterly, 5*(1), 129–142.

Schein, E. H. (1992). *Organizational culture and leadership* (2nd ed.). San Francisco: Jossey-Bass.

Schein, E. H. (1996). Three cultures of management: The key to organizational learning. *Sloan Management Review, 38*(1), 9–20.

Schein, E. H. (1999). *The corporate culture survival guide: Sense and nonsense about culture change.* San Francisco: Jossey-Bass.

Sendjaya, S. (2005). Morality and leadership: Examining the ethics of transformational leadership. *Journal of Academic Ethics, 3*(1), 75–86.

Sendjaya, S., Pekerti, A., Härtel, C., Hirst, G., & Butarbutar, I. (2014). Are authentic leaders always moral? The role of Machiavellianism in the relationship between authentic leadership and morality. *Journal of Business Ethics* http://link.springer.com/article/10.1007/s10551-014-2351-0.

Senge, P. M. (1990). The leader's new work: Building learning organizations. *Sloan Management Review, 32*(1), 7–24.

Sergiovanni, T. J. (1992). *Moral leadership: Getting to the heart of school improvement.* San Francisco: Jossey-Bass.

Sherry, S. B., Hewitt, P. L., Besser, A., Flett, G. L., & Klein, C. (2006). Machiavellianism, trait perfectionism, and perfectionistic self-presentation. *Personality and Individual Differences, 40*(4), 829–839.

Sims, R. R. (1992). The challenge of ethical behavior in organizations. *Journal of Business Ethics, 11,* 505–513.

Thoma, S. J., & Rest, J. R. (1986). Moral judgement, behavior, decision making, and attitudes. In J. R. Rest (Ed.), *Moral development: Advances in theory and research* (pp. 133–175). New York: Praeger.

Trevino, L. K., & Brown, M. E. (2004). Managing to be ethical: Debunking five business ethics myths. *The Academy of Management Executive, 18*(2), 69–81.

Trevino, L. K., Hartman, L. P., & Brown, M. (2000). Moral person and moral manager: How executives develop a reputation for ethical leadership. *California Management Review, 42*(4), 128–142.

Turner, N., Barling, J., Epitropaki, O., Butcher, V., & Milner, C. (2002). Transformational leadership and moral reasoning. *Journal of Applied Psychology, 87*(2), 304–311.

Weiss, H. (1977). Subordinate imitation of supervisory behavior: The role modeling in organizational socialization. *Organizational Behavior and Human Performance, 19,* 89–109.

Wyld, D. C., & Jones, C. A. (1997). Importance of context. The ethical work climate construct and models of ethical decision-making – An agenda for research. *Journal of Business Ethics, 16,* 465–472.

Yukl, G. (1990). *Leadership in organizations.* Englewood Cliffs: Prentice-Hall.

Transcendental Spirituality

7

> *We are not human beings having a spiritual experience. We are*
> *spiritual beings having a human experience.*
> (Pierre Teilhard de Chardin)

Of the six dimensions of servant leadership, *Transcendental Spirituality* is perhaps the most contested one. Critics say spirituality should be confined to private spaces and has no academic merit and contributions to the public sphere. Bringing spirituality into the workplace, if anything, will generate more problems rather than solutions it is purported to offer. Contrary to these dissenting views, we have seen a proliferation of research on workplace spirituality since the 1990s (Dale 1991; Fairholm 1997, 1998; Fry 2003; Hawley 1993; Holland 1989; Kunde and Cunningham 2000; Mitroff and Denton 1999b). A cursory review of the literature would yield many definitions of the construct. Giacalone and Jurkiewicz (2003, p. 13) offer perhaps the most comprehensive understanding of the construct:

> A framework of organizational values evidenced in the culture that promotes employees' experience of transcendence through the work process, facilitating their sense of being connected in a way that provides feelings of compassion and joy.

According to the above definition, leaders who foster spirituality in the workplace will create a culture where employees experience three things: a sense of transcendence, interconnectedness, and meaning. These three indicators are not mutually exclusive. They complement each other such that one could potentially experience all three when spirituality as a core value flourishes in the organization. Such culture is worth cultivating because the positive effects workplace spirituality has on leaders, followers, and organizations, including better leadership (Conger 1994), improved ethical behavior (Fort 1995), increased creativity (Biberman and Whittey 1997), improved productivity (Nash 1994), higher employee effectiveness and reduced absenteeism and turnover (Giacalone and Jurkiewicz 2003), and increased

© Springer International Publishing Switzerland 2015
S. Sendjaya, *Personal and Organizational Excellence through Servant Leadership,*
Management for Professionals, DOI 10.1007/978-3-319-16196-9_7

job performance (Neck and Milliman 1999). In fact, spirituality has been heralded as a new competitive advantage (Mitroff and Denton 1999b).Servant leadership is often considered synonymous with spiritual leadership (Fairholm 1997; Korac-Kakabadse et al. 2002). Servant leaders are spiritual in the sense that their lives are driven by a sense of higher purpose and meaning, and project an alignment between the internal self and the external world. They possess inner consciousness and sense of mission, and are attuned to the idea of calling in seeking to make a difference in the lives of others through service (Sendjaya et al. 2008). *Transcendental Spirituality* is thus defined as behaviors of the leader which manifest an inner conviction that something or someone beyond self and the material world exists and makes life complete and meaningful. There are four values of *Transcendental Spirituality*, namely transcendental beliefs, interconnectedness, sense of mission, and wholeness.

7.1   Transcendental Beliefs

Modern organizations are often ambivalent towards its members possessing a religious or spiritual belief. This tendency stems by and large from the fear that subscribing to such belief will lead to problems such as workplace proselytizing, favoritism, and discrimination. Interestingly, instead of witnessing the disappearance of religion and spirituality the last two decades have seen a proliferation of religious-infused or spiritual-based practices in various workplace settings. This trend should not come as a surprise given the continuing decline of trust that people have towards the external world that no longer give them meaning, direction, and security. Many grow disillusioned by the vicious cycle of high unemployment and inflation, increasing gaps in wealth and power, and perpetual scandals of once trustworthy government and business leaders. As these external indicators are growing dim, they stop turning outward to catch a glimpse of hope, certainties and direction, instead they turn either upward towards someone or something higher than themselves (religion) or inward towards their inner self (spirituality).

Mitroff and Denton (1999a) maintain that broadly speaking there are four attitudes towards religion and spirituality. First, a positive view towards both religion and spirituality. This attitude conveys that true spirituality is experienced and developed only through religion. Leaders with this view derive their strength and inspiration from the spiritual experience within the boundaries of their respective religious teachings and rituals. Second, a positive view towards religion but negative towards spirituality. People who subscribe to this view have a strong belief in the teaching and rituals of a particular religion which dictates their moral performance and preferences. They have religion without spirituality which is merely an ideology that one along with like-minded people identifies with collectively.

Third, a negative view towards religion but positive towards spirituality. According to this view, religion is exclusive, close-minded, and intolerant whereas spirituality is universal, open-minded, and tolerant. They possess spirituality without religion. Finally, a negative view towards both religion and spirituality. People show this attitude because of the belief that everything worthwhile in the modern secular workplace should be confined by the boundaries of scientific methods, anything beyond that is considered outdated and irrelevant.

A cursory review of the literature on spiritual leadership reveals that an overwhelming majority of leadership scholars seem to favor the third view. As such, spirituality is often defined in opposition to religion in order to avoid any potential divisive conflicts arising from a vast range of religious beliefs or practices (Hicks 2002; Korac-Kakabadse et al. 2002). Hicks (2002), for example, argues that religion is typically perceived as institutional, dogmatic, and rigid whereas spirituality is seen as personal, emotional, and adaptable to an individual's needs. He and other proponents of this view more often than not conclude with the truism that 'spirituality unites, but religion divides'.

Needless to say going into the religion-spirituality debate is simply beyond the scope of this book. My experience, observation, and study however led me to conclude that having a transcendental belief, that is a volitional belief in something or someone higher than one self. This belief entails more than a mere intellectual assent but a conviction that guides one's development of priorities, decisions, and behaviors. It stems from the awareness that there is more to life than meets the eye, and as the above quote opening this chapter shows, we are essentially spiritual beings with material needs rather than the other way around.

I would like to propose three reasons why both religious and spiritual beliefs are powerful transcendental drivers for servant leaders. First, despite the prevalence of the third view above, other leadership scholars maintain that spirituality cannot be utterly detached from religiousness (Fairholm 1997), primarily because spirituality is historically rooted in religion (Cavanagh 1999). Carter (1993) contended that the detachment of spirituality from religion is attributed to the tendency of people, particularly in the western world, to trivialize religion merely as an unproductive emotional outlet which has no relevance to public life, an attitude which downgrades the real significance of religious beliefs in both public and personal actions. While Fry (2003) maintained that spiritual leadership may or may not embrace religious theory and practice, he found that most literature on spiritual leadership come from the field of religious theology (e.g. Banks and Powell 2000; Blackaby and Blackaby 2001; Ford 1991; Sanders 1994; Wright 2000).

Allport (1950) operationalized the motivational dimension of religiousness in terms of Intrinsic and Extrinsic Religiousness. Intrinsic religiousness is demonstrated when one treats religion as religion as a meaning-endowing framework in terms of which all of life is understood, and hence relates to and integrates every aspect of life. In contrast, extrinsic religiousness is shown when one uses an a self-serving, instrumental means to achieve comfort, social acceptance, and other more transient goals (Donahue 1985), and is often treated as an escape mechanism that leads to a compartmentalized and immature life. Servant leaders are driven by the intrinsic use of religious beliefs.

Second, our reluctance to embrace religious beliefs is indicative of the plausibility structure we put ourselves under. Plausibility structure is a concept developed within the domain of social scientific study of religion. It is operational when the question of why and how individuals regard their belief as real or true is no longer entertained but merely assumed as a given. In this socially constructed realm of what is plausible and implausible, religion is seen essentially as a body of fixed doctrine and ethics subscribed by profoundly insecure people to feel superior to those who do not conform so that their insecurity can be bolstered. The argument typically continues by pointing out that history is replete with examples how adherents of religious beliefs directly and indirectly contribute to exclusion, alienation, and oppression. The conclusion therefore is that religion is bad. But the ensuing decision to deem religion implausible and jettison it altogether is akin to throwing the proverbial baby with the bathwater.

In his seminal work *The Gulag Archipelago 1918–1956,* Aleksandr Solzhenitsyn, a survivor of Stalin's concentration camp and recipient of 1970 Nobel Prize for Literature, argued that the fault is not in the religion itself, because the line that separates good and evil does not pass through states, classes, or religions, but right through the human heart. His oft-quoted statement captured this sentiment (1974, p. 168):

> If only it were all so simple! If only there were evil people somewhere insidiously committing evil deeds, and it were necessary only to separate them from the rest of us and destroy them. But the line dividing good and evil cuts through the heart of every human being. And who is willing to destroy a piece of his own heart?

Third, if we care enough to stop and reflect honestly on our own experiences, we are essentially spiritual beings with an innate need to derive a sense of meaning and connectedness from something or someone higher than ourselves. This 'something' or 'someone' is often what drives leaders to wake up early in the morning and jump into action doing what he or she deeply believes is called to do. While financial independence and power might be a powerful driver, the most inspiring and effective leaders know the hollowness of such motive. Both religious and spiritual beliefs give that more profound sense that there is a higher power beyond us whose influence guides one's actions and with whom one has a relationship (Block 1993; Fairholm 1997).

This lesson was learned early by David Steward, founder and CEO of World Wide Technology, a multi-billion dollar systems integrator that provides technology and supply chain solutions, towards the end of his decade-long career in sales for three Fortune 500 firms (Steward 2004). He recalled the epiphany he had when was awarded Salesman of the Year at a Federal Express national sales meeting and invited to the stage to receive an ice bucket with his initials engraved. When he looked inside the bucket and found out it was empty, what he thought was a peak success experience made him question what he really wanted in life. Reflecting on that defining moment, he decided to start World Wide Technology on a tiny budget as a platform for ministry rather than wealth accumulation. He credited the success of the company to his belief in God and a commitment to serve others, and shared that philosophy in a church program *Doing Business by the Book* attended by a wide spectrum of people including governors, senators, congressman, and other dignitaries.

An increasing number of business leaders have reportedly been relying on their religious beliefs, values, and practices for business solutions and leadership approaches (Delbecq 1999; Mitroff and Denton 1999b; Nash 1994). Reave (2005) chronicles a few business leaders whose leadership experience and success are drawn from or attributed to spiritual insights. Tom Chappel, owner of Tom's of Maine, a personal care products company, found within himself a sense of emptiness despite the success of his business. He decided to enrol into Harvard Divinity School. The insights gleaned from his training to transform the company into one with a strong stewardship model built around core values of natural, sustainability, and responsibility, which set the standard for every decision they make every day. Kris Kalra, CEO of BioGenex, a medical-lab technology business, was an extreme workaholic before he decided to embark on spiritual retreat for 3 months. After rediscovering that lost sense of higher purpose, he returned to work and found himself leading a much more meaningful life and successful business with 12 new patens and sales growth. My own research suggests a similar sentiment, as the following quote by a seasoned director of a leadership training firm indicates:

> Spiritual value is a deeper reason why people lead as servant leaders. You can't teach them in MBA courses that value simply to have a better bottom. It really comes from somewhere deeper in the person. If you do, in the end, they'll revert. They'll revert, and they exercise their power themselves. That's what all human beings do. Unless there are some overriding spiritual value things that push them in the other direction.

7.2   Interconnectedness

The notion of interconnectedness is well integrated within the realm of spirituality and well documented in the literature, as shown in the following definitions of spirituality:

- "An awareness within individuals of a sense of connectedness that exists between inner selves and the world." (Stamp 1991, p. 80).
- "The basic feeling of being connected with one's complete self, others, and the entire universe" (Mitroff and Denton 1999b, p. 83).
- "A source guide for personal values and meaning-making, a way of understanding the world, an inner awareness. It is a means of integration of the self and our world." (Fairholm 1997, p. 25).
- "The feeling individuals have about the fundamental meaning of who they are, what they are doing, and the contributions they are making" (Vaill 1998, p. 218).

The above definitions suggest that central to human experience is the need to have a sense of alignment, of being aware that the personalities, competencies, and capabilities one has can be a significant contribution to the world (Csikszentmihalyi 2003). Interconnectedness, therefore, refers to the inner belief that one's giftedness fits the work that he or she does. Interconnectedness signifies a deeply reciprocal interaction between what is inside and outside of us (Palmer 1998). This longing to express the inner self in ways that fit the external world has long been advocated by ancient philosopher Aristotle who argued that one's vocation is found at the point where one's talents and the needs of the world cross. Csikszentmihalyi's (1975, 2003) research revealed that such sense of alignment makes work intrinsically meaningful and motivating, and therefore transcendental in nature. This optimal experience is described as 'flow experience' (Csikszentmihalyi 1975, p. 36):

> A unified flowing from one moment to the next, in which he is in control of his actions, and in which there is little distinction between self and environment, between stimulus and response, or between past, present, and future.

A servant leader has a sense of being connected in that they know exactly why they choose a certain career or job as their choice reflects the talents and preferences they believe are endowed to them for a purpose. That purpose is much higher than the fancy titles, salaries, and perks they might receive. As such, servant leaders believe that their lives are not as a series of random events, but their family background, temperaments, training, life experiences are knit together to prepare them to be the very people best fit for the work. Palmer (2000, p. 5) reflects this trajectory when he wrote:

> Vocation does not mean a goal that I pursue. It means a calling that I hear. Before I can tell my life what I want to do with it, I must listen to my life telling me who I am. I must listen for the truths and values at the heart of my own identity, not the standards by which I must live – but the standards by which I cannot help but live if I am living my own life

Servant leaders is driven by a sense of that calling, reflecting a conviction that they are being intellectually, psychologically, emotionally, socially, and spiritually qualified to produce excellent results in what they do. This sense of alignment between one's self and one's occupation creates an intrinsically stimulating and rewarding career. A group executive of one of the largest charity organizations in the world remarks his comment below the importance of this self-awareness as a building block for one's engagement with the world:

> I think if you believe that there's a God, then you actually have come to the point where you realize that you're part of something that is bigger than you. You then question the part that you're supposed to be playing. That's what drives me because I know I'm at the right place. I really feel fortunate because the right place for me is in a position that really changes peoples' lives. I had some personal experiences where you realize that what you do in 9 to 5, you've actually seen the results of it in somebody's life elsewhere in the world. You realize that you have a huge indirect effect on people thousands of miles away. You should believe that that's what God wants you to do.

7.3   Sense of Mission

The third element of spirituality, sense of mission, is basic to the human condition. Berger (1967, p. 22) asserted that humans are "congenitally compelled to impose a meaningful order upon reality." The intrinsic drive to find meaning and purpose is evident in the workplace, particularly since work occupies an increasing portion of waking hours for most people and is increasingly becoming a central part of their existence (Giacalone and Jurkiewicz 2003). People seek ways to express their spirituality at work by engaging in work that is meaningful and gives them a sense of purpose (Pfeffer 2003). The antithesis of this state is meaninglessness, often experienced by those who feel they make little or zero contribution to the final outcomes of a project.

In fact, work itself has been considered a calling or vocation, which provides a sense of vitality and purpose to business leaders. Delbecq (1999) found many senior executives in his study regarded business leadership as a calling to service, not merely a job or a career. The idea of calling and meaningful work is best summed up by Buechner (1992, p. 189) who asserted that "the place God calls you to is the place where your deep gladness and the world's deep hunger meet." The Bible itself contains stories of ordinary individuals being called to lead by God in various secular posts serving their fellow citizens. Joseph was a top-ranking Minister of Logistics in Egypt. Nehemia was Project Manager in charge of the rebuilding of the Jerusalem Wall. Lidya was a businesswoman in the garment industry. All these people worked in their field as a response of the calling God gave them. In these examples, what they do in the world with a strong sense of mission from God is not considered inferior to what the clergies do in places of worship.

In summary, being a servant leader is not about doing big things in big ways making big waves for everyone to see, but becoming a positive influence in the roles they have been providentially called and stationed. The fulfillment of that calling is manifested in the experience of making a difference in the lives of others through service. Servant leaders help others to generate a sense of meaning out of everyday lives at work, interpreting social realities with the shared values people deeply believe in. As meaning-makers, servant leaders assist them to find clarity of purpose and direction. The following comments illustrate the attribute of *Sense of Mission*:

> To significantly contribute to the alleviation of poverty among those who suffer throughout the world, especially children. That's what's driven me for the last 20 years, and it's what's driven me within this organization and what keeps me going everyday. I think the servant leadership approach is much more congruent with that particular mission than different styles of leadership (male, group executive, charity).

7.4   Wholeness

The scientific management approach of organizations which created the division of labor and specialization has elicited a sense of isolation and alienation in the workplace (Aktouf 1992; Bolman and Deal 1995). The following lament, often attributed to the American industrialist Henry Ford circa 1930s though the originality remains unconfirmed, still rings very true today, "Why do I always get a whole person, when all I want is a pair of hands?" Many workplaces view employees as part of their 'human resources', and just like physical assets that organizations have, they are expendable. Treating them as a means to an end, rather than an end in and of themselves, would therefore be justified.

The Taylorism approach to production suggests that human beings like computers whom they can turn on at the start of the day and off at the end of the day. As automatons, their value lies in what they can produce, and their needs, dreams, and hopes are often sacrificed on the altar of performance and growth. This disconnectedness of self from others in and outside the workplace has evolved into compartmentalization of life. In turn, compartmentalization of life into separate domains (e.g. work, family, religion, and social obligations) inevitably leads to a fragmented life characterized by disparate relationships which clouds personal meaning and purpose in life (Fairholm 1997; Mitroff and Denton 1999a). The fragmentation of life has created a vacuum within the overwhelming majority of professional workers marked by unproductive stress and numbing emptiness. In the words of philosopher Henry David Thoreau, they lead lives of 'quiet desperation', going through motions with a hunger for meaning and purpose.

Servant leaders are fully aware that people are not human resources, but human beings, and that they are much more than the sum of their outputs. They are holistic individuals with an intellectual side, a physical side, an emotional side, a moral side, and a spiritual side, and each needs to be acknowledged and given equal attention. Hicks (2002) highlights the need for people to bring their whole selves to the workplace without any distinctions between public and private lives, spiritual and physical realms, and sacred and secular dimensions. In their empirical study, Sarros et al. (2002) found that leadership positively contributes to meaningful workplaces marked by the absence of work alienation. Spiritual-based servant leadership given its holistic outlook is fitting for the very purpose of restoring the lost sense of wholeness. The following echoes this sentiment:

> Servant leadership is about inviting the human element into the workplace because you recognize that you are working with people, not things. It helps people to have a sense of completeness in life. And the more we have that sense of completeness within us in the workplace, the more we are likely to contribute to the organization, and hence, the better the organizational performance is.

7.5   Actionable Commitments of Servant Leadership

The following commitments are practical outworking of the *Responsible Morality* dimension. As with other commitments, they are part of the servant leadership behavior scale (SLBS) whose psychometric properties have been well established.

Commitment #25 – Am driven by a sense of a higher calling
Do you live for something that will outlast you? If you feel you are trapped in the here and now, take some time off to examine whether your commitments reflect your

calling. If you have the resources, you can hire people to do anything you don't like doing but there is you cannot delegate the task of discovering your calling. A calling is the consciousness that you are compelled to some special task, equipped to do it well, and shown opportunities to enter it.

Commitment #26 – Help others to generate a sense of meaning out of everyday life

Help others to see that hardwired within us is a strong desire for life to mean something. Let them think that while they may not believe in life after death or any religious belief, they cannot escape the longing for a sense of meaning that is not bound by time and space. They can of course deny it but will end up living their lives in quiet desperation. If it is within your prerogative, start routine offsite sessions to get people to take a helicopter view of their work and life. This can be a three-hour session every three months when everyone identifies the meaningless from the meaningful habits or things they do at work. Ask them thought-provoking questions such as one that Steve Jobs used to apply to himself, "If today were the last day of my life, would I want to do what I am about to do today?". Something has to change if the answer is 'no' for a few days in a row.

Commitment #27 – Help others to find a clarity of purpose and direction

Challenge others to think in specific ways how they want to leave this world in a better condition than when they found it. Ask them to write their own eulogy to get them to think how they want to be remembered by others. Instill a strong sense of mission within them. If there is a gap between their life purpose and daily priorities, ask them to stick with their life purpose and alter their priorities, not vice versa. Help them build a practice saying no to those 'once-in-a-lifetime opportunities' that seem to keep coming more often in one's life.

Commitment #28 – Promote values that transcend self-interest and material success

Share with others how the world gears us into a lifestyle of having too much to live with and too little to live for. Tell stories like that of a successful investment banker who lamented in his 65th birthday how he spent his entire life stepping up the corporate ladder only to find that the ladder is leaning against the wrong wall. Most importantly, model a life that demonstrates there is something else far more valuable than material success.

References

Aktouf, O. (1992). Management and theories of organizations in the 1990s: Toward a critical radical humanism. *Academy of Management Review, 17*(3), 407–431.

Allport, G. W. (1950). *The individual and his religion: A psychological interpretation.* New York: Macmillan.

Banks, R., & Powell, K. (2000). *Faith in leadership.* San Francisco: Jossey-Bass.

Berger, P. (1967). *The sacred canopy: Elements of a sociological theory of religion.* Garden City: Doubleday.

Biberman, J., & Whittey, M. (1997). A postmodern spiritual future for work. *Journal of Organizational Change Management, 10*(2), 130–188.

Blackaby, H., & Blackaby, R. (2001). *Spiritual leadership*. Nashville: Broadman & Holman.

Block, P. (1993). *Stewardship: Choosing service over self-interest*. San Francisco: Berrett Koehler.

Bolman, L. G., & Deal, T. E. (1995). *Leading with soul*. San Francisco: Jossey-Bass.

Buechner, F. (1992). In G. O'Conner (Ed.), *Listening to your life*. San Francisco: Harper.

Carter, S. (1993). *The culture of disbelief*. New York: Basic Books.

Cavanagh, G. F. (1999). Spirituality for managers: Context and critique. *Journal of Organizational Change Management, 12*(3), 124–134.

Conger, J. A. (1994). *Spirit at work: Discovering the spirituality in leadership* (1st ed.). San Francisco: Jossey-Bass.

Csikszentmihalyi, M. (1975). *Beyond boredom and anxiety: The experience of play in work and games*. San Francisco: Jossey-Bass.

Csikszentmihalyi, M. (2003). *Good business: Leadership, flow, and the making of meaning*. London: Hodder & Stoughton.

Dale, E. (1991). *Bringing heaven down to earth: A practical spirituality at work*. New York: Peter Lang.

Delbecq, A. L. (1999). Christian spirituality and contemporary business leadership. *Journal of Organizational Change Management, 12*(4), 345–349.

Donahue, M. J. (1985). Intrinsic and extrinsic religiousness: Review and meta-analysis. *Journal of Personality and Social Psychology, 48*(2), 400–419.

Fairholm, G. W. (1997). *Capturing the heart of leadership: Spirituality and community in the new American workplace*. Westport: Praeger.

Fairholm, G. W. (1998). *Perspectives on leadership: From the science of management to its spiritual heart*. Westport: Quorum.

Ford, L. (1991). *Transforming leadership: Jesus' way of creating vision, shaping values and empowering change*. Downers Grove: InterVarsity Press.

Fort, T. L. (1995). The spirituality of solidarity and total quality management. *Business and Professional Ethics Journal, 14*(2), 3–21.

Fry, L. W. (2003). Toward a theory of spiritual leadership. *The Leadership Quarterly, 14*, 693–727.

Giacalone, R. A., & Jurkiewicz, C. L. (2003). Toward a science of workplace spirituality. In R. A. Giacalone & C. L. Jurkiewicz (Eds.), *Handbook of workplace spirituality and organizational performance* (pp. 3–28). New York: M.E. Sharp.

Hawley, J. (1993). *Reawakening the spirit in work: The power of dharmic management*. San Francisco: Berrett Koehler.

Hicks, D. A. (2002). Spiritual and religious diversity in the workplace: Implications for leadership. *The Leadership Quarterly, 13*(2), 379–396.

Holland, J. (1989). *Creative communion: Toward spirituality of work*. New York: Paulist Press.

Korac-Kakabadse, N., Kouzmin, A., & Kakabadse, A. (2002). Spirituality and leadership praxis. *Journal of Managerial Psychology, 17*(3), 165–182.

Kunde, J., & Cunningham, B. (2000). *Corporate religion*. London: Financial Times Management.

Mitroff, I. I., & Denton, E. A. (1999a). A study of spirituality in the workplace. *Sloan Management Review, 40*(4), 83–92.

Mitroff, I. I., & Denton, E. A. (1999b). *A spiritual audit of corporate America: A hard look at spirituality, religion, and values in the workplace*. San Francisco: Jossey-Bass.

Nash, L. (1994). *Believers in business*. Nashville: Thomas Nelson.

Neck, C., & Milliman, J. (1999). Thought self-leadership: Finding spiritual fulfilment in organizational life. *Journal of Managerial Psychology, 9*, 9–16.

Palmer, P. J. (1998). Leading from within. In L. C. Spears (Ed.), *Insights on leadership: Service, stewardship, spirit, and servant leadership* (pp. 197–208). New York: Wiley.

Palmer, P. J. (2000). *Let your life speak: Listening for the voice of vocation*. San Francisco: Jossey-Bass.

Pfeffer, J. (2003). *Business and the spirit*. New York: M.E. Sharp.

Reave, L. (2005). Spiritual values and practices related to leadership effectiveness. *The Leadership Quarterly, 16*, 655–687.

Sanders, O. J. (1994). *Spiritual leadership*. Chicago: Moody Press.

Sarros, J. C., Tanewski, G. A., Winter, R. P., Santora, J. C., & Densten, I. L. (2002). Work alienation and organizational leadership. *British Journal of Management, 13*, 285–304.

Sendjaya, S., Sarros, J. C., & Santora, J. C. (2008). Defining and measuring servant leadership behaviour in organizations. *Journal of Management Studies, 45*(2), 402–424.

Solzhenitsyn, A. I. (1974). *The Gulag Archipelago, 1918–1956: An experiment in literary investigation*. Scranton: HarperCollins.

Stamp, K. (1991). Spirituality and environmental education. *Australian Journal of Environmental Education, 7*(1), 79–86.

Steward, D. (2004). *Doing business by the Good-Book: Fifty two lessons on success straight from the Bible*. New York: Hyperion.

Vaill, P. B. (1998). *Spirited leading and learning: Process wisdom for a new age*. San Francisco: Jossey-Bass.

Wright, W. C. (2000). *Relational leadership: A biblical model for influence and service*. Cumbria: Paternoster.

Transforming Influence

8

If you think you're too small to have an impact, try going to bed with a mosquito in the room. (Anita Roddick)

Transforming Influence, the sixth and final dimension of servant leadership, is the behaviors of the leader that help employees to be what they are capable of becoming. Central to the idea of servant leadership is its transforming influence on the individuals who work with and around the servant leader. The word *transformation* comes from two ancient Greek words *meta* and *noia,* both of which are still used in the English language today (e.g., *meta*morphosis and para*noia*). When combined the two words literally mean 'above the mind', referring to the idea of stretching beyond the boundaries within which we normally process reality. In short, a paradigm shift.

Such paradigm-shifting influence that servant leaders have on their followers can be observed in terms of their beliefs, values, and practices. Their work orientation for example is profoundly altered from "how I use my talents to benefit me in every single possible way" to "how I understand myself well enough to discover the best way to use my gifts to serve others." Their perception of power evolves as they no longer operate out of the notion "I control all the power", rather "I share power to build team strength and cohesiveness". They no longer entertain the self-orientated mentality that "everyone should listen to me because I am better", and embrace the Emersonian thinking "I should listen to others more because everyone I meet is my superior in some way." What these examples highlight is these followers do not just improve under the leadership of servant leaders. They have not improved, but they have been deeply transformed. At the end of the day, remarked De Pree (1989, 14), servant leaders leave a different sort of legacy, that is one that "takes into account the more difficult, qualitative side of life, one which provides greater meaning, more challenge, and more joy in the lives of those whom leaders enable." More specifically, servant leaders' transforming influence have three distinct characteristics:

© Springer International Publishing Switzerland 2015
S. Sendjaya, *Personal and Organizational Excellence through Servant Leadership*,
Management for Professionals, DOI 10.1007/978-3-319-16196-9_8

1. *The object: Transforming for the sake of followers*

   In the servant leadership economy, followers are transformed not for the sake of the organizational bottom line but for their own development and growth. Their increased motivation and commitment will benefit them first and foremost, when and if the organization benefits that would be a natural by-product of empowered followers. Graham (1991) argues that this emphasis on the followers' own good sets servant leadership apart from other theories like transformational leadership. The latter is often construed as a manipulative form of leadership that energizes followers to achieve performance beyond expectations for the sake of the leader or shareholders but not necessarily the followers.

2. *The direction: Transforming followers in multiple dimensions*

   Greenleaf (1977, p. 27) argued that servant leadership is demonstrated whenever the people who are served by servant leaders are positively transformed in multiple dimensions, including emotionally, intellectually, socially, and spiritually: "Do they, while being served, become healthier, wiser, freer, and more autonomous, more likely themselves to become servants?" As such, followers are not merely turned in a mini-me version of the leader. They are not even evolved into a better version of themselves. Rather they are empowered to become what they are capable of becoming when each dimension of their individual self is fully explored and developed.

3. *The method: Transforming the organization, one follower at a time*

   Needless to say, leaders need to be able to influence the crowd through public speaking, team meetings, social media, and other means. Servant leaders are not an exception, however, real and significant impartation of vision occurs primarily in the context of one-on-one meetings. Thus they always create and leverage on the opportunities to engage people in personal, one-on-one encounters. Greenleaf (1977) implies that servant leadership is contagious, that is in the course of working together with servant leaders, followers are transformed into servant leaders themselves. This intentional method of transforming one follower at a time, however, produces something quite remarkable. The contagion effect does not merely nurture additional servant leaders, it multiplies them. It is the difference between showing people how to fish and modelling them how to fish in such a way that inspires to do the same to others. Suppose a servant leader reaches out to 100 people every day in an attempt to influence them to be servant leaders, she would reach 36,000 people in the first year, 72,000 in the second year, 180,000 in the fifth year, and 360,000 in the tenth year. But if the same leader puts all her energy and attention to only four people for the entire first year, these four people will be energized and enabled to do the same and together transform 16 people into servant leaders in the second year. At the end of the first decade, there will be 1,048,576 servant leaders! As this multiplier effect of personal transformation occurs, it stimulates positive changes in organizations and societies (Russell and Stone 2002).

Starbucks CEO Howard Schultz was often cited for his passion to create an organization where its members are treated with dignity and respect. Under his leadership, Starbucks became the first company in the United States which offers comprehensive health insurance and stock options ownership to every employee including part-time workers. Starbucks also invests heavily in humanitarian causes initiating programs like funding loans to small businesses, hiring veterans and spouses of active-duty military personnel who face unemployment rate, and contributing more than 54,000 volunteer hours in housing projects in the wake of natural disasters like Hurricane Katrina. These initiatives were not an employee motivation scheme reengineered to boost the company profit but to ensure that employees are ethically, psychologically, and emotionally empowered to make a positive difference in the society.

There are five sub-dimensions of servant leaders' transforming influence, each of them provides a set of distinct means by which servant leaders bring about deep and lasting changes in the lives of others. These means are vision, empowerment, modeling, mentoring, and trust. In other words, servant leaders transform their followers to be servant leaders by casting vision, empowering, role modeling, mentoring, and trusting them.

8.1 Vision

Servant leadership is closely associated with the idea of vision because in the course of serving others a servant leader "needs to have a sense for the unknowable and be able to foresee the unforeseeable" (Greenleaf 1977, pp. 21–22). Vision is typically understood as a clear mental image of a preferable future seen by the leader but invisible to others. Vision is crucial for both individuals and organizations because it links the present to the future, energizes people, builds commitment, provides meaning to work, and establishes a standard of excellence. Collins and Porras (1997) offered a framework for vision which comprises two complementary elements: core ideology and an envisioned future. Core ideology includes the core values and purpose of the organization which must never change, whereas the envisioned future consists of the organizational operating practices and business strategies which must be open for change. While it is important for leaders to hold a desired future state in mind, they also need to have an accurate picture of current reality. The gap between the two creates a creative tension (Senge 1990), which becomes the fuel on which the engine of transformation is run.

While leaders in all shapes and sizes must have a clear vision, the vision that servant leaders casts is rather unique in the following sense:

The Vision Fuels and Guides the Service Granted the first priority of servant leaders is to serve others, yet they do not serve merely to satisfy their individual needs and aspirations, let alone their personal preferences or whims. Servant leaders are not doormats for people to trample on. In fact, the perception that servant leadership has no greater purpose other than to serve others is simply flawed. When servant leaders treat followers with unqualified acceptance, it does not mean that followers are encouraged to remain stuck where they are or be anything other than what they aspire to do. Rather in the course of seeking to transform others to be more servant-like, servant leaders role model these behaviors through service. Thus, servant leaders' vision is leader-centric rather than follower-centric.

This is manifested clearly in the life of Jesus Christ whose life revolves around the vision of bringing people into the kingdom of God. His servant leadership was demonstrated when he sought to influence others to pursue that vision yet chose the path of servanthood to achieve it. His ultimate accountability however is to his heavenly Father. Similarly, servant leaders in contemporary organizations exist to serve others, but they are accountable to the board of directors and other stakeholders and bound to the vision and values of the organization. As such they would say to their followers, "I am your servant, but you are not my master. I am here to serve you to be what you are capable of becoming such that our shared image of the future is achieved."

The Vision Is a Shared Vision Senge (1990) pointed out the importance of a shared vision to which organizational members can be truly committed. Many leadership visions are merely top-down visions of the CEO or the top management team that trigger responses ranging from apathy to grudging or formal compliance. More specifically, Senge (1990, p. 9) wrote:

> When there is a genuine vision (as opposed to the all-too-familiar 'vision statement'), people excel and learn, not because they are told to, but because they want to. But many leaders have personal visions that never get translated into shared visions that galvanize an organization. All too often, a company's shared vision has revolved around the charisma of a leader, or around a crisis that galvanizes everyone temporarily.

Given the impression management skills leaders have at their disposal, many run the risk of over-exaggerating their visions to appear more realistic or more appealing than they actually are. This superiority trap often spells failure on the leaders' part to receive feedback that might be critical to the achievement or sustainability of the vision (Conger 1991). A shared vision is different because each individual can see him or herself in it and is excited to be part of it. Followers who feel they have a stake in the shared vision will not only help achieve it but also remind the leader that the vision is bigger than the leader. Servant leaders create a compelling shared vision for everyone working with them. They take into account the aspirations of many into the creation of such vision. They articulate the shared vision in such a way that many not only understand it but are inspired to participate in it. The servant leader's central task, therefore, is to turn personal vision to a shared vision which energizes and excites people.

The Vision Creates Volunteers The late Peter Drucker, the Father of Modern Management, taught that the best employees work like volunteers (Cohen 2009). If they are treated like volunteers, i.e., they are free to leave at any time, the leader cannot strictly rely on financial incentives to retain or motivate them. Rather the leader must impart a clear vision in such a compelling way that the vision becomes so attractive they want to dedicate their time and energy into it. A compelling vision is the reason why millions of individuals give nearly 5 h each week to non-profit organizations. Herb Kelleher, former CEO of Southwest Airlines, one of the most admired employers in the US, understands the power of a compelling vision in building a culture of commitment. His employee-focused vision, built around the concept of love (the company's stock ticker symbol is *luv*), continues to attract thousands to apply to work for the company. In the words of Kelleher (1997, p. 21):

> Financial analyst once asked me if I was afraid of losing control of our organization. I told him I've never had control and I never wanted it. If you create an environment where the people truly participate, you don't need control. They know what needs to be done, and they do it. And the more that people will devote themselves to your cause on a voluntary basis, a willing basis, the fewer hierarchs and control mechanisms you need. We're not looking for blind obedience. We're looking for people who on their own initiative want to be doing what they're doing because they consider it to be a worthy objective. I have always believed that the best leader is the best server. And if you're a servant, by definition you're not controlling

The Vision Outlasts the Leader Servant leaders do not draw their identity and self-esteem from the success of achieving that vision. They understand that intoxicating power of vision; first the leader manages the vision, then the vision manages the leader. On the contrary, whenever leaders who see themselves synonymous with the vision, the organization is bound to have succession issues which more often than not will lead to its demise. It is sobering to note that the average life expectancy of multinational corporations is between 40 and 50 years (De Geus 1997). While their short life expectancy can be attributed to a range of factors, corporate leaders are often the primary usual suspect. The irony is some leaders brought the company the founded down with them to make a point that they are uniquely indispensable. Drucker (1990, p. 15) in his vintage style is instructive on this point:

> The worst thing you can say about a leader is that on the day he or she left, the organization collapsed. When that happens, it means the so-called leader has sucked the place dry. He or she hasn't built. They may have been effective operators, but they have not created the vision. Louis XIV was supposed to have said, *L'etat, c'est moi!* (The state, that's me!). He died in the early eighteenth century and the long, not-so slow slide into the French Revolution immediately begun.

8.2 Empowerment

Empowerment is considered a key characteristic of servant leadership (Buchen 1998; Pollard 1996; Russell and Stone 2002). Blanchard (1998, p. 28) asserted that servant leadership is about "making goals clear and then rolling your sleeves up and doing whatever it takes to help your people win." This view is shared by Wilkes (1998, p. 27) who claimed that "servant leaders multiply their leadership by empowering others to lead." As such, servant leaders possess a commitment to and derive satisfaction from the growth of others, believing that people have an intrinsic value beyond their contribution as workers or employees.

In practical terms, empowerment is shown most visibly in organizations when there is a delegation of decision making responsibility to those close to the internal and external customers or stakeholders, the process of which includes giving away power from the central coordination of the organization to people at the lower levels of the organization (Conger and Kanungo 1988). For the process to effectively occur, leaders who gives away the power distribute their authority and should take it back from the people who receive it only when necessary and as a last resort. Conger and Kanungo (1988, p. 474) provided a more prescriptive definition of empowerment as:

> A process of enhancing feelings of self-efficacy among organizational members through the identification of conditions that foster powerlessness and through their removal by both formal organizational practices and informal techniques of providing efficacy information.

Hence, empowerment can be perceived either as a motivational construct (power as an intrinsic need for self-determination) or relational construct (the perceived power that an individual or unit has over others), although the former refers to an enablement process, not just delegation (Conger and Kanungo 1988). In summary, empowerment implies responsibility, autonomous decision-making, power sharing, and feelings of self-efficacy.

Servant leaders prioritize followers' growth and development and build a positive culture of continual learning where everyone engages in a developmental trajectory from their first day in the company. At Zappos.com, CEO Tony Hsieh prefers to grow talents from within and puts every new recruit through a 4-week training program. There are 30 different courses that are accessible to every employee including tribal leadership, public speaking, stress management, and introduction to finance. At the end of the first week, the new recruits are offered $2,000 to quit and they have 3 weeks to decide before the training concludes.

The way servant leaders empower their followers is unique in that they unconditionally accept people as they are yet expect them to go the extra mile. Followers are willing to push themselves harder because they know of they have been fully accepted by the leader despite their track record. Thus they perform beyond the call of duty not to get the servant leader's nod, rather because the servant leaders have approved and trusted them they are empowered to excel. A CEO in the interview study put it as follows:

> I really want to push people to achieve that they didn't realize they could've achieved and to do things in a way that perhaps they didn't realize they could do. At the same time, I don't want to push people so hard that they burn out or they're destroyed as a person. I think that's just incredibly counterproductive. We'll get a far better result if we have people that are cared for on the one hand, but are being stretched on the other hand.

8.3   Modelling

Researchers concur that role modeling, or setting a personal example in visible and tangible ways, is an important element of servant leadership (Batten 1998; De Pree 1992; Pollard 1996; Russell and Stone 2002). As role models, servant leaders provide a standard of behaviour and values for others to imitate. They understand that the most powerful way to communicate a vision is by embodying it, personifying it, living it out. When servant leaders display behaviors that are aligned with such vision, followers are bound to emulate the desired behaviors. The motivational effects of leadership role modeling has been traditionally explained by Bandura's (1977, p. 35) social learning theory which suggests that our behavioral patterns emerge following observation and imitation of others in a social context:

> By observing a model of the desired behavior, an individual forms an idea of how response components must be combined and sequenced to produce the new behavior. In other words, people guide their actions by prior notions rather than by relying on outcomes to tell them what they must do

As intimated above, servant leaders begin with a leader-centric, shared vision that elevates followers in multiple dimensions. Their primary way to garner followers' commitment around that vision is to model ideal behaviours. In his discussion of primary and secondary embedding mechanisms of culture, Schein (1999, p. 98) argues that of all strategies leaders can navigate to shape and change culture, the most important is leaders' visible behaviours which reflects what they "pay attention to, measure, get upset about, reward, and punish." What leaders do in practice is far more vital in determining the culture than what they espouse, publish, or preach. In practical terms, servant leaders transform others through mentoring by engaging their followers in the art of apprentice training involving the following steps: (1) I do. You watch. We chat; (2) I do. You help. We chat. (3) You do. I help. We chat, (4) You do. I watch. We chat; and (5) You do. Someone else watches. This continuous process preserves that the contagion effects of servant leadership at various levels of the organization, hence effectively turning organizations into leadership factories.

8.4   Mentoring

Mentoring is generally defined as an interpersonal relationship where a mentor guides others who are inexperienced or less senior to them to achieve personal and professional goals (Ehrich and Hansford 1999), hence is more systematic and intensive than modeling because it requires time, energy, and commitment. In the context where leaders are increasingly evaluated based on the number of leaders they develop instead of merely the number of followers, mentoring is an important strategy for leadership effectiveness (Wheatley 1999). The benefits of mentoring for the mentor, mentee, and organization have been well documented. Some of the key benefits of mentoring for a mentee includes career advancement, personal support, increased learning and development, higher productivity, and reduced stress levels (Cobb and Gibbs 1990; Cunningham 1993). As for mentors, the benefits include career rejuvenation, personal fulfillment, and assistance on projects (Ehrich and Hansford 1999).

Unfortunately, many talented individuals in organizations are either underdeveloped or overlooked or both because leaders are too preoccupied with their more urgent and important tasks that they have little time to mentor others. They become prisoners of their own routines, furiously running the organizational machine that needs feeding and constant attention. In such scenario, it is only natural for leaders to pay attention to the mature and able followers who put their professional lives ahead of their personal and family lives. While it might be fitting for these star-performers to get all the attention and rewards they deserve, often leaders miss an important pool of talents when they neglect the B players who make up the overwhelming majority of organizational members. DeLong and Vijayaraghavan (2003) contend that B players are often neglected because while they consistently exhibit steady performance quietly, they do not attract public attention when they succeed.

Critics of the rank-and-yank system that over-simplistically labels employees as A, B, and C players abound. However rather than putting a moratorium on this performance management framework, it is perhaps temper it with logic and prudence. Mentoring only A players however will not be a smart and sustainable leadership development strategy because of the following two reasons. First, the lower performance of B players relative to that of A players often reflects something other than their ability such as low person-job fit or unsupportive team culture. Second, A players perform highly often for self-oriented motive such as money, power, prestige, and would instinctively quit the organization once they sense that their agenda is better served elsewhere. Rather than focusing on solely the A players, DeLong and Vijayaraghavan (2003) recommend leaders to create a culture that recognizes, appreciate the contributions of every employee and assist them to deliver A performance. The practical tips in the box below would help servant leaders to choose whom to mentor.

Who Stole My Passion?

MacDonald (1986) contends that there are five different types of people in any organization, a category which I find practically useful in identifying the potential mentees (as well as mentors) for servant leaders. It would be prudent to

(a) Very Resourceful People (VRP) are people who will *ignite* the passion within the servant leader to attain excellence and keep that passion going.

(continued)

They pull from the front, cheer on from the side, and push from behind to help servant leaders operate at an optimum level without burning out.

(b) Very Important People (VIP) are those who *share* the passion, speaking at the same wavelength and laboring alongside the servant leaders to achieve a mutually shared goal.

(c) Very Trainable People (VTP) are those who *catch* the passion, demonstrating a desire to learn and a teachable spirit to grow and develop. These people are prime candidates for future leaders.

(d) Very Nice People (VNP) are those who *enjoy* the passion that servant leaders exhibit but never have the intention to commit themselves into it. While they are fun to be around with, their interest in becoming servant leaders or contribution to the vision is low. Their kindness should not be confused with their commitment.

(e) Very Draining People (VDP) are those who *sap* the passion, needy users who demand the servant leaders to invest time and energy and leave them dry at the end of the day. Granted servant leaders should not ignore VDPs, some of them may become VTPs or even VIPs, but VDPs should be allowed to crowd the agenda and drains the resources of the leader.

Check your calendar to see who has been receiving your time and attention. Then consider whether you felt that you have gained or lost energy in your interactions with them. Think of the changes you ought to make to ensure that you invest a significant portion of your time and energy mentoring VTPs and being mentored and reinvigorated by VRPs and VIPs.

Servant leaders mentor others not for the benefits they would get. Rather, because they see themselves as a steward, someone who is entrusted with individuals who work closely with and around them to be nurtured and developed into what they are capable of becoming. However, rather than focusing on the benefits they receive as mentors, servant leaders mentor others to transform and multiple themselves. Servant leaders might inspire hundreds or thousands of people in the organization and beyond, but they would strategically choose to devote most of their time to a group of select individuals that they take under their wings. They grow dissatisfied by merely functioning as leaders of followers, even if they are quite efficient and effective at that. Rather, they choose to become leaders of leaders. To that end, they serve others through a mentoring relationship in which they:

(a) become good students of their individual followers, seeking to understand their needs, whether they are intellectual, emotional, or spiritual in order to support them as they carry it, and encourage them along the way,

(b) discipline themselves to listen attentively to their aspirations and dreams rather than opening their mouth at every opportunity to advertise their stream of consciousness,
(c) are willing to have their lives complicated by the struggles of their followers without impatience or complaint in order to help remove the burden,
(d) provide candid feedback about followers' performance in the most constructive way,
(e) intensively ask thoughtful questions to push them beyond their boundaries, and
(f) challenge and clarify their preconceived notion of their personal values and beliefs.

By making the above part of their daily priority, servant leaders draw the best out of others, making enormous and strategic contributions to followers' personal and professional growth, and in the end raise them up as leaders.

8.5   Trust

In an era where organizational restructuring and downsizing is prevalent, fostering trust in the workplace can be a tough challenge for corporate leaders. Nevertheless, building trust in organizations is the primary responsibility of leaders, and particularly important in the eyes of followers. The importance of trust in organizational leadership is also highlighted by Bennis and Nanus (1985, p. 153) who remarked that "the accumulation of trust is a measure of the legitimacy of leadership. It cannot be mandated or purchased; it must be earned." More prescriptively, Rousseau et al. (1998, p. 395) provided a multidisciplinary definition of trust: "Trust is a psychological state comprising the intention to accept vulnerability based upon positive expectations of the intentions or behavior of another."

While the notion of trust is not exclusively attached to servant leadership and may be considered a key element in virtually all leadership models, servant leadership has been strongly associated with trust in the literature (De Pree 1997; Joseph and Winston 2005; Melrose 1995; Patterson 2004; Russell 2001). Greenleaf (1977, p. 25) asserted that trust lies at the root of servant leadership. Given their internal secure sense of self, servant leaders are willing to be vulnerable in front of their followers, which in turn instill followers' trust and confidence in their leaders. The extent to which a leader is trustworthy depends largely on the extent to which followers can predict the leader's decision or action when facing a dilemma based on the pattern shown in the past. Servant leaders are predictable because they "translate personal integrity into organizational fidelity" (De Pree 1997, p. 127). They follow through with what they said they would do, and when fail never come up with elegant excuses. They never wonder what their followers are doing when they are not around to check on them and never fear that they are being manipulated or taken advantage of in any way. They do not flatter, lie, manipulate, or deceive in any way in order to co-opt their followers into doing what the leaders want. Because of the reciprocal trust shown by their followers, they do not see the need to edit their words or withhold their feelings in front of them.

Jack Lowe (1998), CEO of TDIndustries, a US-based mechanical contractor ranked as one of the best companies to work for by *Fortune* magazine (Levering and Moskowitz 2001), maintained that servant leadership is the foundation of trusting relationships in the organization. A high-trust culture among employees provides an organization with an agility to respond to the constantly changing business environment without having to hassle with constant internal resistance to change (Lowe 1998). At the more individual level, Lowe (1998) proposed that there are two ways leaders establish relationships with new recruits, namely by treating them with suspicion until they prove themselves trustworthy or assuming that they are trustworthy until they prove otherwise. Servant leadership has enabled him to choose the latter. The capacity to trust others even when the risks are great is an expression of emotional wisdom on the part of servant leaders (Bennis and Nanus 1985).

8.6 Actionable Commitments of Servant Leadership

The following commitments relate to the *Transforming Influence* dimension. As with other commitments, they are part of the servant leadership behavior scale (SLBS). Get two or three people who work closely with you to give you informal feedback on how you do on the following behaviors, and ask them to suggest a few practical ways for you to excel.

Commitment #29 – Articulate a shared vision to give inspiration and meaning
One of the greatest legacies that you can leave others is a vision that will outlast generations of leaders. That shared vision should be much bigger than you. You are the steward of that vision, owning it, growing it, achieving part of it, and then passing it onto the next generation of servant leaders. Intentionally spend one-on-one quality time with individuals in the organization to understand the current reality they face and the future reality they long for. If their journey from current to future reality can be embedded within the vision, they would catch and own it too.

Commitment #30 – Minimize barriers that inhibit others' success
Amabile and Kramer (2011, p. 22) in their study on what motivates employees the most based on hundreds of diary entries concluded that "of all the things that can boost emotion, motivation, and perceptions during a workday, the single most important is making progress in a meaningful work." As such, support others in their daily progress towards a shared vision by removing obstacles to success. The obstacles can be a rigid organizational structure, narrow performance-appraisal system, over-competitive culture, or even unsupportive supervisor. They can be hierarchical or structural, real or imagined. Routinely ask, "Is there anything that might stop you from becoming better at who you are and what you do, and what can I do to knock those barriers down?" Get to the root cause, and not just the symptoms, of those hindrances.

Commitment #31 – Contribute to others' personal and professional growth
How approachable are you as a leader? Do your direct reports come to you for personal and professional advice? Do you know them well enough to know their struggles and hopes? Build a system of accountability in which each person is accountable to someone for his or her personal and professional growth.

Commitment #32 – Lead by personal example
Lead by personal example at every point in the journey towards a shared vision. At times you may be found in front of the pack to show the path. Sometimes you may need to walk alongside others to share the ups and downs of the journey. Yet occasionally you are most needed at the very back to encourage people to carry on in the journey. If you are constantly with them in the thick of action, they will know you are a predictable and hence trustworthy leader.

Commitment #33 – Inspire others to lead by serving
De Pree (1989:11) wisely observed that "the first responsibility of the a leader is to define reality. The last is to say thank you. In between, the leader is a servant." When you serve others in big and small ways, do it in secret. If you call a press conference, it will never inspirational and transforming. But when you catch others exemplifying servant leadership in their attitudes, behaviors, or initiatives, recognize them in a very public manner.

Commitment #34 – Draw the best out of others
In the servant leadership economy, the ultimate function of leadership is to produce more leaders, not followers. If servant leaders are surrounded by people more talented than they are, they should breed servant leaders who are better than they are.

Commitment #35 – Allow others to experiment and be creative without fear
When leaders expect employees to be creative but punish them when they make mistakes, people instinctively learn at least two things: That leaders only pay lip service and that playing safe is more important than taking risk. As such, mean what you say when you encourage your staff to experiment and push boundaries, and to make honest mistakes faster than others. Granted they would one day make that costly blunder, and when that happens, speak frankly yet gently to debrief them. The goal of course is not to find a scapegoat, attack one's character or assault his intelligence. Rather ask constructive questions such as, "What lessons can we learn from this blunder? What does it tell us about us? How can we ensure the next mistake we make is not this same one but a new one?"

References

Amabile, T. M., & Kramer, S. J. (2011). The power of small wins. *Harvard Business Review, 89*(5), 70–80.
Bandura, A. (1977). *Social learning theory.* Englewood Cliffs: Prentice Hall.

Batten, J. (1998). Servant leadership: A passion to serve. In L. C. Spears (Ed.), *Insights on leadership: Service, stewardship, spirit, and servant leadership* (pp. 38–53). New York: Wiley.

Bennis, W. G., & Nanus, B. (1985). *Leaders: The strategies for taking charge.* New York: Harper & Row.

Blanchard, K. (1998). Servant leadership revisited. In L. C. Spears (Ed.), *Insights on servant leadership: Service, stewardship, spirit, and servant leadership* (pp. 21–28). New York: Wiley.

Buchen, I. H. (1998). Servant leadership: A model for future faculty and future institutions. *Journal of Leadership Studies, 5*(1), 125–134.

Cobb, J., & Gibbs, J. (1990). A new competency-based, on the job programme for developing professional excellence in engineering. *Journal of Management Development, 9*(3), 60–72.

Cohen, W. A. (2009). *Drucker on leadership: New lessons from the father of modern management.* San Francisco: Jossey-Bass.

Collins, J. C., & Porras, J. I. (1997). *Built to last: Successful habits of visionary companies.* New York: Harper Business.

Conger, J. A. (1991). The dark side of leadership. *Organizational Dynamics, 19*(1), 44–55.

Conger, J. A., & Kanungo, R. N. (1988). The empowerment process: Integrating theory and practice. *Academy of Management Review, 13*, 471–482.

Cunningham, J. B. (1993). Facilitating a mentorship programme. *Leadership and Organization Development Journal, 14*(4), 15–20.

De Geus, A. (1997). *The living company: Habits for survival in a turbulent business environment.* Boston: Harvard Business School Press.

De Pree, M. (1989). *Leadership is an art.* New York: Doubleday Publishing.

De Pree, M. (1992). *Leadership jazz.* New York: Dell Publishing.

De Pree, M. (1997). *Leading without power: Finding hope in serving community.* San Francisco: Jossey-Bass.

DeLong, T. J., & Vijayaraghavan, V. (2003). Let's hear it for B players. *Harvard Business Review, 81*(6), 96–102.

Drucker, P. (1990). *Managing the non-profit organizations.* New York: Routledge.

Ehrich, L. C., & Hansford, B. (1999). Mentoring: Pros and cons. *Asia Pacific Journal of Human Resources, 37*(3), 92–107.

Graham, J. (1991). Servant-leadership in organizations: Inspirational and moral. *Leadership Quarterly, 2*(2), 105–119.

Greenleaf, R. K. (1977). *Servant leadership.* Mahwah: Paulist Press.

Joseph, E. E., & Winston, B. E. (2005). A correlation of servant leadership, leader trust, and organizational trust. *Leadership and Organization Development Journal, 26*(1), 6–22.

Kelleher, H. (1997). Building a culture of commitment. *Leader to Leader, 4*, 20–24.

Levering, R., & Moskowitz, M. (2001, January 8). The 100 best companies to work for in America. *Fortune*, 148–168.

Lowe, J. (1998). Trust: The invaluable asset. In L. C. Spears (Ed.), *Insights on leadership.* New York: Wiley.

MacDonald, G. (1986). *Restoring your spiritual passion.* Nashville: Thomas Nelson.

Melrose, K. (1995). *Making the grass greener on your side: A CEO's journey to leading by serving.* San Francisco: Berrett-Koehler.

Patterson, K. (2004). *Servant leadership: A theoretical model.* Paper presented at the Servant Leadership Research Roundtable, Virginia Beach, VA.

Pollard, C. W. (1996). *The soul of the firm.* Grand Rapids: Harper Collins.

Rousseau, D. M., Sitkin, S. B., Burt, R. S., & Camerer, C. (1998). Not so different after all: A cross-discipline view of trust. *Academy of Management Review, 23*(3), 393–404.

Russell, R. F. (2001). The role of values in servant leadership. *Leadership and Organization Development Journal, 22*(2), 76–83.

Russell, R. F., & Stone, A. G. (2002). A review of servant leadership attributes: Developing a practical model. *Leadership and Organization Development Journal, 23*(3), 145–147.

Schein, E. H. (1999). *The corporate culture survival guide: Sense and nonsense about culture change.* San Francisco: Jossey-Bass.

Senge, P. M. (1990). *The fifth discipline: The art and practice of the learning organization.* New York: Doubleday.

Wheatley, M. J. (1999). *Leadership and the new science: Learning about organization from an orderly universe.* San Francisco: Berrett-Koehler.

Wilkes, C. G. (1998). *Jesus on leadership: Discovering the secrets of servant leadership from the life of Christ.* Wheaton: Tyndale House.

Servant Leadership Development

As highlighted in the previous chapters, servant leadership is a holistic approach to leadership that engages both leaders and followers through six dimensions (*Voluntary Subordination, Authentic Self, Covenantal Relationship, Responsible Morality, Transcendental Spirituality, and Transforming Influence*) such that they are both transformed into what they are capable of becoming. As such servant leadership development also takes into account the development of both the leaders and followers from a holistic perspective.

An effective leadership development program strikes a balance between leader and leadership development orientations in order to cover facets of personal and organisational challenges (Day et al. 2004; McCauley and Velsor 2004). The 'leader development' orientation assumes an individualistic view of leadership, in which leaders are clearly distinguished from followers, whereas the 'leadership development' orientation treats leadership as a distributed property by which every person is a leader. The former emphasizes on individual based knowledge, skills, and abilities associated with formal leadership roles (e.g., self-awareness, personal ethics), the latter building interpersonal competence in a social context (e.g., influencing others, leading through chaos). Both developmental orientations however are insufficient in that they neglect equally important areas such as morality and spirituality.

Given the pervasiveness of morally flawed corporate leaders, the need to reflect on and think through moral decisions in ill-defined and ethically ambiguous environments cannot be overstated as it will spell success or failures for the organisations and their stakeholders. The notion that the exercise of authority and power always entails ethical challenges (Hollander 1995) must be part of the perennial topics for discussion. Servant leadership development programs encompass morality and spirituality development by exposing leaders and potential leaders to a range of scenarios where they are confronted with ethical dilemma, conflicts of interest, organizational politics, and leadership crisis. The emphasis on morality and spirituality fills the void in leadership training industry that is fixated

© Springer International Publishing Switzerland 2015   117
S. Sendjaya, *Personal and Organizational Excellence through Servant Leadership,*
Management for Professionals, DOI 10.1007/978-3-319-16196-9_9

on the organizational performance and growth often at the expense of staff. The goal of these leadership development programs typically is to enhance employees' self-efficacy to make a bigger sacrifice for the sake of the bottom line. In the process of doing so, employees are treated as means to an end (i.e., human resources) rather than an end in themselves. Their emotional, ethical, and spiritual sides that make up who they are often get neglected. Servant leadership programs provide an alternative approach as they focus on employees, helping them to develop a sense of meaning and wellbeing as well as shaping their moral awareness and emotional maturity.

Rather than going over the details of the programs which go beyond the scope of this chapter, I will focus on the organizing framework of servant leadership development. Figure 9.1 shows the three triangles of servant leadership development, each representing different developmental strands. The first is the Leaders-Followers-Context triangle, signifying the object of servant leadership development. Rather than focusing on the leader, servant leadership fosters a leader-follower relationship that elevates both the leaders and followers, and such relationship occurs in a supporting culture that fosters learning and growth. The second triangle shows that servant leadership development will help leaders and followers to re-interpret their past, reimagine their future, and re-align both with their present self. As such, the journey to become servant leaders is purposeful, meaningful, and life transforming.

Fig. 9.1 The three triangles of servant leadership development

The third triangle deals with the three important inflection points, namely being, knowing, doing, all of which need to be balanced and interwoven to each other. Each of these triangles is in turn elaborated below.

9.1   The Leaders-Followers-Context Triangle

A servant leadership development initiative may start with the servant leader but it is also oriented towards empowering the leader to better serve others because servant leaders exist not for their sake but for the sake of others, that is as stewards to grow and develop those they serve to be what they are capable of becoming. The program should also enables the servant leader to be an organizational architect to build cultures, structures, and systems within which the servant leadership philosophy is embedded, thus creating a conducive environment where service, authenticity, intimacy, morality, spirituality, and transformation flourish in leader-follower relationships. In summary, servant leadership development programs should equally address three key elements of leadership – leaders, followers, and context.

That leadership is an intricate interplay among leaders, followers, and context has been well documented in the literature. In a field replete with definitions, nearly as many as those who study it, the best ones include all three elements. Rost (1991, p. 102), for example, concludes from his study of leadership definitions that leadership is "an influence relationship among leaders and followers who intend real changes that reflect their mutual purposes." The strength of this definition lies in the dynamic exchanges between leaders and followers that occur in a context of a shared commitment to achieve a mutual goal. For a leadership process of relationship to occur, leaders need followers and vice versa. Leadership is always a two-way traffic. Similarly, the role of context is critical to leadership. Cawthorn (1996, p. 3) captures it well using an example of two historical figures: "Without the chaos in the Roman Catholic Church, would Lutheranism exist today? Without racial tension in the United States, would Martin Luther King have remained an obscure minister in the South?" Granted one can forever debate the old-age topic of whether leaders shape context (e.g., Carlyle's (1888) view that history is the biography of great men) or context shapes leaders (e.g., Tolstoy's (1869) kings are the slaves of history). But research on leadership and organizational culture has found strong evidence in support of both views. While leaders play pivotal roles in creating, nurturing, and changing the organization's culture, the culture of an organization also affects the development of leadership (Schein 1999). The development program should assist servant leaders translate their conviction in the ideals of servant leadership into everyday routines and reinforce them using personal examples and other means such that a multiplier effect within the organization organically occurs.

Since genuine and deep learning is best done relationally, as servant leaders are taught to serve and develop others they would learn new things about themselves. Since an important part of learning to understand ourselves consists of looking into what drives us into anger, anxiety, and pain, the leader-follower interaction can be a rich source of learning for leaders. The following sample questions can be used to facilitate learning in this space, and the ensuing reflection on the part of the leader would reveal something about the leader's motives and approach:

- To what extent do you involve your followers in developing plans, making strategic decisions, allocating resources, solving problems, managing conflicts, and handling crises?
- In the course of involving them, are your followers being used to serve your agenda, or are you empowering them to use their talents more productively?
- Do you derive more satisfaction from having the task completed which help boost your career or knowing your followers become more emotionally mature and ethically proficient as a result?
- What do you want to get out of leading others? What's in it for you?

9.2   The Past-Present-Future Triangle

Leadership development programs which center around a cookie-cutter leadership style are bound to be ineffective because each individual is unique. Even identical and fraternal twins have different trajectories of leadership development (Zhang et al. 2009). The goal of leadership development therefore is not to create more clones of Jack Welch or Steve Jobs. These and other household names of corporate leaders were effective in what they do, at least judged from the perspective of the financial side of the respective companies they led, but what their individual approach to success could not necessarily be replicated in different contexts. Each had their individual life stories was uniquely theirs, and we would be remiss to try to imitate them (see Shamir and Eilam (2005) to read further on the life-story approach to leadership). Instead we need to focus on our own life stories, understanding our strengths and limitations. In the words of Young & Rubicam CEO Ann Fudge (cited in George et al. 2007, p. 130): "The challenge is to understand ourselves well enough to discover where we can use our leadership gifts to serve others."

Ancient philosophers from the West and the East have long taught the wisdom of knowing ourselves, from Socrates ('an unexamined life is not worth living') to Lao Tzu ('knowing others is intelligence; knowing yourself is true wisdom'). Research shows that self-awareness is the most essential capability for leaders to develop (George et al. 2007). My experiences in teaching both undergraduate students and senior executives (and anyone in between) over the last decade suggest that the single most important thing about servant leadership development is the capacity to have an intimate understanding one's past, present, and future and synchronizing them to produce a meaningful trajectory of leadership development.

The servant leadership development process therefore is a three-step journey towards self-discovery: Going back (past) into the crucible events in one's life, going forward (future) into one's vision of an ideal future, and going inward (present) into one's core values. This is critical for servant leaders because they must (a) in relation to the past reach out to and redeem their emotional scars and/or psychological neuroses to have a secure sense of self to be able to abandon themselves to the strengths and expectations of others, (b) in relation to the present be fully aware of their functional rather than professed values to help themselves and others navigate a moral maze, and (c) in relation to the future possess a clear and focused vision to be able to make it a shared vision that transform others to be servant leaders. There is a tremendous value, and personal relief, in experiencing that 'a-ha' moment when the servant leader feels that everything falls into its place. That occurs when they come to grip with the reasons behind, means for, and ends of their choice to lead by serving.

An overwhelming majority of leadership programs teach leaders to evaluate their present and navigate their future, but rarely do these programs assist leaders to revisit and reframe their past. It is fitting therefore to focus our discussion on how servant leadership development programs can help leaders to do the latter. Understanding the past is important for every leader because one's childhood experiences have profound influences in shaping leaders (e.g., Avolio and Vogelgesang 2011; Bennis and Thomas 2002; Murphy 2011; Murphy and Johnson 2011). Research on determinants of leadership suggests that as much as 70 % of the variance in leadership role occupancy can be attributed to environmental factors (Arvey et al. 2006). The finding highlights among others the importance of significant early years experiences that powerfully shape leaders. Children who experience higher parental support and lower conflict with parents, for example, are likely to have leadership opportunities that are determined more by environmental rather than genetic factors (Zhang et al. 2009). On the contrary, children with undermining parents are more likely to be abusive supervisors (Kiewitz et al. 2012). Verbal abuse in particular is a lethal form of undermining as it has a higher chance to be readily passed onto between generations relative to physical forms of abuse (Ney 1987).

9.2.1 The Past

9.2.1.1 Early Years Experience

Sinclair (2007) argued that early years experiences often encourages or discourages leadership because they shape one's appetites for and vulnerabilities around leadership. The appetites, desires, and neuroses that we learned early in our family color and shape our career ambitions and the preferred means to achieve them. Consider the pattern observed in destructive leaders like Stalin, Pol Pot, Hitler, Mussolini, and Mao, all of which had very dark childhood memories including the experience of being alienated, estranged, and/or abused. Price (2005) argued that these peculiar formative circumstances became a sort of special education on the attainment and maintenance of power and domination. Ludwig's (2002 as cited in Price 2005, p. 68) outlines the traumatic experiences endured by the 'infamous five' as follows:

> Joseph Stalin's father, who periodically beat him and his mother, was a violent alcoholic and was eventually killed in a brawl when Stalin was eleven years old. Pol Pot's parents sent him to live with an older brother and his wife, who adopted him when he was six, so his relationship with his parents was distant or resentful at best, despite his brother's claim

about the lack of open conflicts with them. Adolf Hitler's father, who died when he was
eight, drank heavily and was brutally violent toward his family. Mussolini's father drank
too much, womanized, and was intermittently employed. Mao Zedong hated his father for
beating him and his brothers and for shaming him in front of others, and constantly bucked
his authority.

In a similar vein, Stien (2007) maintains that both Ken Lay and Jeff Skilling, the
former chairman and CEO of Enron, respectively, grew up with a version of Oedipus
complex where an intense struggle a son and his father shaped their formative
years. In the absence of a father's authority and emotional support, these two
boys separately found themselves in situations where they had to take premature
responsibilities for their family. Slowly an inner desire developed within them
to replace the father. The Oedipal mindset remained unresolved throughout the
adulthood and culminated at the peak of their career when as powerful executives
they undermined and eliminated at will employees who reminded them of their
father. In fact, Stien (2007) even suggests that Lay and Skilling perceived the
government and regulatory authorities as a weak father figure who became a threat
to their personal ambition to succeed.

9.2.1.2 Crucibles

The main lesson drawn from the above life stories is not that traumatic childhood
experiences create destructive leaders, but that left unchecked and unredeemed
these experiences would animate the dark side of leaders' souls. Servant leadership
development programs would in fact help leaders to reframe their past beyond their
formative years into what Bennis and Thomas (2002) call 'crucibles'. Named after
the ancient vessels used by alchemists to turn base metals into gold, crucibles are
intense, transformative, defining moments which compel people to question their
identity, values, priorities, and assumptions such that they arrive to a new or altered
sense of self. While these crucibles can be positive, most of them are negative
and can include a range of events such as peer rejection, parental abuse, career
disruption, supervisor bullying, marital breakdown, death of loved ones, and so on.
In the final analysis, Bennis and Thomas (2002, p. 39) conclude that "one of the most
reliable indicators and predictors of true leadership is an individual's ability to find
meaning in negative events and to learn from even the most trying circumstances."
Problems, not projects, make leaders.

As such, the most salient issue to ponder in servant leadership development
programs revolves around how to best leverage the effects of dark experiences in
the lives of the participants for their learning such that they go away better rather
than bitter. Indeed the same sun that melts the wax hardens the clay. The same trial
of life that shapes one to be an effective and ethical leader may mold another person
to become a dysfunctional and unethical leader. The experience of being betrayed,
for example, may turn someone into a leader who does not trust his followers and
manipulate them to achieve his ambition, yet the same experience may trigger in
another leader a conviction to intentionally foster a deep and genuine relationship
with his followers (i.e., *Covenantal Relationship*).

Many potential leaders become more Machiavellian precisely because they are trained to employ superficial charm to manipulate others to their advantage. They behave in a chameleon manner, changing their shape at will to suit their surrounding out of self-preservation or self-profit motives. Sherry et al. (2006) found that Machiavellianism correlates positively with perfectionistic self-presentation, that is they are adept at projecting an image of superiority in areas that are expected to them. Their chameleon-like repertoire may propel them to, for example, appear authentic for the sake of expediency. Carl Jung (2000) once warned that "the brighter the persona, the darker the shadow."

The rise and fall of the civil rights activist Rev Jesse Jackson is instructive on this point. Widely perceived as a moral compass by the American public, Rev Jackson fought for many human rights issues for various minority groups both nationally and internationally. The public perception of his *Authentic Self* (i..e, someone with integrity, humility, accountability) saw him run for the U.S. president twice, and drew President Clinton to him. As a spiritual adviser and close confidant, he provided counsel to President Clinton at the peak of the Monica Lewinsky scandal in 2001. Later he himself became the national headline news when the public learned that he fathered a love child around the same time the presidential affair occurred.

What turns a servant leader like Rev Jackson into a Machiavellian? My studies, observation, and experiences led me to believe that whatever else the answers are, it can be attributed to the absence of the capacity to deal with one's pains, wounds, or deprivation in the past. Clinical research on leadership has long established that "the past is the lens through which we can understand the present and shape the future" (Kets De Vries and Korotov 2012, p. 267). The wounds we carry from our past become a lens through which we interpret the world even when we claim we see things as they truly are. In fact, the things that we fail to remember are probably things that impact us most profoundly. Some of these scars are quite traumatic we hide them in the dark recesses of our soul and hope that they remain locked away. But they jump right back at us unexpectedly in the presence of the right stimuli.

Servant leadership development must take into account these crucibles, helping leaders to admit and acknowledge the potential dark side which affect their leadership practice more profoundly than they realize. It is sobering for servant leaders to take a guided trip down the memory lane to connect the dots among those seemingly meaningless negative experiences and reflect on how they have shaped the leaders today. Pain can become a fertile soil for either the most destructive or constructive sides of a leader (Goodman 2007). For servant leaders, these painful experiences become a tremendous source of clarification and understanding of the path of service they choose.

The programs will not and cannot change their past, but helps them to redeem its meaning and embrace the next crucible coming their way with a more resilient outlook and positive response. As such, they would learn that their best leadership lessons are learned not at a business school but at the school of hard knocks. Crucibles might knock them down, but they would refuse to be knocked out. Instead they would initiate a Socratic dialog with themselves, extract lessons on the essence of leading through service, drawing further strength for their distinctive leadership path. Bennis (1989, p. 61) wisely wrote:

> We cannot change the circumstances of our childhood, much less improve them at this late date, but we can recall them honestly, reflect on them, understand them, and thereby overcome their influence on us. Withdrawal can be turned to hope, compulsion to will, inhibition to purpose, and inertia to competence through the exercise of memory and understanding.

9.2.2 The Present

Redeeming the past is therefore key to understanding why we are driven by certain ambitions and live by certain values. Those who were deprived of love, attention, approval, or power will spend their entire lives seeking these things and make them their core values. Core values are those that bind the existence of someone that make life worth living and leadership worth doing. These values compete, and leaders have to choose a set of core values by which other values are judged. Core values exercise preeminence over other values in guiding the leaders' decisions and actions. More often than not these values – approval, control, comfort, achievement – begin as a means to power enabling the leader to control but then overpower and control the leader.

The following self-diagnostic questions will help servant leaders to identify their core values:

- What do I daydream about? Where does my mind drift instinctively?
- What do I want to be known that makes me proud?
- What keeps me awake at night? What do I worry about?
- What do I fear losing the most that would make me feel I cannot face tomorrow?
- When things go bad or get difficult, where do you turn for refuge and comfort?

Servant leadership development programs on core values focus on two objectives. First, they help leaders reflect on their core values and subject them to a reality check. Subconsciously leaders give those values the authority to guide and justify their decisions and actions. Often unbeknownst to the leaders, these values control them by capturing their imagination in the form of vivid, ideal image of a future they believe make their lives meaningful and significant. For example, leaders whose core values include achievement tend to think, "Life is meaningful only if am being recognized for my accomplishments in this leadership role." If materialism is their core value, they would be driven to seek financial freedom and certain level of wealth, "My worth is solely based on the status symbols I possess around me." Still if approval is their value of choice, they would say, "What's the point of my life is I am not respected by those people who matter to me?"

Life always has a way to abruptly take those things that we hold dearly away from us. Global financial crisis can end one's leadership career or vaporize one's financial wealth in a matter of days, for example. Relationship breakdowns have been known to ruin the lives of approval-oriented people. As such, to cultivate *Authentic Self,* servant leaders must realize that what they highly value can be snatched from them rather unexpectedly. It is insufficient for leaders to know that accomplishment, materialism, or approval make up their core value. They need to question whether they are truly a reliable and sustainable guide and seriously reconsider which values are worth holding onto as core values.

The second objective is gauge to what extent these values are truly core, functional value. Every senior executive at Enron knew by heart the four famous corporate values – Respect, Integrity, Communication, and Excellence. However they also knew that they are just a part of a motherhood statement since in reality the only value that matters is the maximized price per share of common stock. A simple exercise similar to the one offered by Sull and Houlder (2005) will be useful to examine the extent to which how the leaders spend their time, money, and energy matches their core values. The point of the exercise is to identify the gap between the two, following which participants can either reorder their commitment or reconsider their values.

9.2.3   The Future

Similarly leaders' vision is often tied strongly to their past. Starbucks CEO Howard Schultz's vision to build Starbucks as a company that treats people with dignity and respect was largely born out of the impression he had growing up in a working class family. Years of helplessly witnessing his dad struggling with a stint of blue-collar jobs and offered no worker's compensation or health insurance cover when he was injured on the job forms a strong desire for him to build company that his father never had the luxury of working for. Indeed vision often begins with a strong sense of discontentment with the status quo both in the past and present, which over time grows, evolves, and matures into an increasingly clear picture of what could be. But it remains a potential until it gives birth to a conviction such that something that *could be* done becomes something that *should be* done. Anything less is a compromise. The gap between what is and what could be is what Senge calls a creative tension. Such creative tension catapults servant leaders like Martin Luther King, Jr. (1963) into tireless acts of service to his countrymen, as made clear in the letter he wrote from the Birmingham city jail:

> Just as Socrates felt it was necessary to create a tension in the minds of men so that individuals could rise from the bondage of myths and half-truths ⋯ we must see the need of nonviolent gadflies to create the kind of tension in society that will help men rise from the dark depths of prejudice and racism to the majestic heights of understanding and brotherhood.

Servant leaders should be taught to think through a creative tension that propels them to lead others and choose the path of less travelled road of service to achieve the vision. Without such creative tension, they will not be able to exert *Transforming Influence* on others. And when the creative tension is felt and shared by others, both the leaders and followers would experience ahead of time the positive emotions associated with the anticipated future. These emotions fuel their present day commitment to the vision, give meaning even to the most menial and tedious task attached to the vision, and maintain their resilience whenever a setback occurs.

9.3   The Being-Knowing-Doing Triangle

Effective leadership development always consists of three foundational elements – being, knowing, doing. The three elements becomes the cornerstone of leadership development of the US Army (2004), the world's largest leadership training organization in the world with the most sophisticated and intensive leadership program. At the West Point Academy, military cadets are taught about being (character), knowing (skills), and doing (action). My theorizing is rather different from that of the US Army as follows. *Being* concerns with the motive behind a particular decision or action, and that decision or action in turn challenges and shapes a leader's initial motive such that a character shift occurs. *Knowing* refers to cognitive mastery of a subject or a field. A leader with a good grasp of knowing is characterized by a deep understanding of why things work they way they are, an ability interpret or estimate realities on the basis of relevant theories, frameworks, models or policies, and a sense-making capacity. *Doing* is essentially focused on the leader's development of skills or abilities which can be task-oriented (e.g., strategic thinking, resource allocation) and people-oriented (e.g., conflict resolution, team building). In summary, *Being* is about character or know-why, *Knowing* is about concept or know-what, and *Doing* is about competency or know-how.

An overwhelming majority of formal leadership programs offered by universities, training institutes, and consulting firms focus on *Knowing*, following by *Doing*. A cursory look at the first year management/leadership subject suggests that students will have to superficially understand approximately 100 management and leadership theories or concepts. To a lesser extent, leadership competencies are developed within formal university settings, hence no surprise they become a major foci of all sorts of non degree-based leadership training and development programs. This covers a wide range of skills from public speaking to scenario planning, from becoming entrepreneurial leader to leading large organizations, and anything in between. To paraphrase an old, familiar joke, here is what leadership development looks like when it is fixated on solely one element:

> Concept is when one knows everything but nothing works.
>   Competency is when everything works but nobody knows why.
>   If concept and competency is combined, nothing works and nobody knows why.

The ugly duckling of leadership development is *Being*. Yet it is the most critical element because leadership flows out of who we are rather than what we know or what we can do. Unlike *Knowing* and *Doing* which have a shorter shelf life in the era of accelerated and perpetual renewal, *Being* is much more permanent and takes a long time to shape or modify. Erich Fromm contrasted being from having when he wrote, "By being I refer to the mode of existence in which one neither has anything nor craves to have something, but is joyous, employs one's faculties productively, is oned to the world"

Examples of one's being include self-concept, core values, ethical orientation, and moral character, all of which do not change every 3 or 6 months. Development of *Being* or character is therefore the most difficult to design and implement relative to development of knowledge and skills, as confirmed in the leadership program at the West Point Academy (US Army 2004). Because it requires a substantial investment of time and resources with little return, the element of character is often neglected within many leadership development initiatives. Needless to say, the dire consequences of this planned neglect can be seen most clearly in the ubiquitous cases of destructive leaders in organizations.

Many seem to be under the impression that formal education, which primarily deals with knowledge and skills, will develop effective leaders. The reality is in the absence of character, formal education despite all the good it delivers has helped create corporate psychopaths or as one author puts it, snakes in suits (Babiak and Hare 2007). An aphorism attributed to author and speaker D.L. Moody aptly puts it as follows: "If you come across a boy who's stealing nuts and bolts from a railway track, and you want to change him, and send him to college, at the end of his education he'll steal the whole railway track." In their study of narcisstic leaders, Rosenthal and Pittinsky (2006, p. 617) maintain that narcissistic leaders possess "a personality trait encompassing grandiosity, arrogance, self-absorption, entitlement, fragile self-esteem, and hostility." While narcissism can be a positive trait that is typically associated with a strong sense of self-esteem or self-confidence and in some cases become the very factor that inspire potential followers (Paunonen et al. 2006), narcissistic leaders who are unable to integrate their grandiose belief systems and self-admiration with their own shortcomings become pathological and destructive. Kets De Vries (1994) contended that this perverse self-love is probably the most salient indicator of defective leadership and usually manifests itself in the leaders' tendencies to manipulate others for their ends, delusional perception that their problems are always unique, addiction to compliments, and demand for special status and entitlements. Enron's CEO Jeff Skilling was a case in point. Convinced that he was the smartest guy in the company, he would dismiss anyone who disagreed with him as stupid because they cannot understand his ideas. He looked down on other energy companies and labelled them 'dinosaurs destined for extinction' and repeatedly claimed that Enron was going bury the competition. Shortly after being lured into Enron, the former McKinsey consultant created a winners-take-all culture within Enron where only the fittest survives (Hamilton and Micklethwait 2006). His narcissism was best shown in his desire to reproduce himself in others by hiring extremely competitive, single-minded MBAs who are willing to work 80 hours a week, a set of attributes which earn them the label 'Skillingites' (Fusaro and Miller 2002).

In their review of management development programs for executives, Kets de Vries and Korotov (2007) argue that many are not transformational because they are oriented towards helping executive doing the same things differently instead of doing different things. For these programs to be truly transformational, they need to be designed to have a lasting emotional-psychological impact addressing the inner theater of the participants, and not just pure intellectual knowledge transfer. This recommendation assumes that both formal leadership programs and real-life experience in leadership are not mutually exclusive, instead they complement each other (Hughes et al. 2005). Accordingly the greatest single contribution of a formal study of leadership provides multiple perspectives from which particular leadership situations and experiences can be analysed. To this end, Kets de Vries and Korotov (2007) developed a triangular framework comprising the mental life triangle (assessing an individual's inner theater which links cognition, emotion, and behavior), conflict triangle (confronting one's hidden feelings, defensive behaviour, and conflict), and relationship triangle (making sense of the link between present relationships and the past). This triangular framework illustrates the importance of the *Being* or *Character* of leaders which should be embedded in the servant leadership development programs.

The three elements of character-concept-competency are equally important for leadership development, hence need to be given the same allocation of weighting in leadership development. In many ways, the way they operate is akin a prescription medicine which contains three active ingredients. If the prescription lacks any of them, not only will it be ineffective, it could also become toxic. Leaders who have good character and superior competencies but very little concept could easily be disoriented and potentially lead others astray. Leaders who have good character and advanced concepts but lacking competencies might be defensive and lethargic in leading others. Leaders with the highest destructive potential however will be those who have superior concepts and competencies yet exhibit character flaws. As alluded to above, these extremely talented and seasoned leaders are typically formidable high-performers with stellar career and charming yet narcissistic personalities.

Servant leadership development is unique because it focuses on character without sacrificing concept and competency. That is to develop as servant leaders is to learn to put others' needs before our own, be and stay humble, to doubt themselves and therefore rely on others to keep them accountable, accept others as they are yet expect them to change and grow, trust others even the risk is great, and so on. These development areas are indicative of strength of character. Because servant leaders seek to transform their followers to be what they are capable of becoming, they would ensure that they grow in the concept and competencies required to excel at what they do.

In summary, servant leadership development focuses on creating holistically healthy leaders and it includes the psychological, intellectual, ethical, emotional, and spiritual elements of the leaders. Quick et al. (2007) maintains that attributes of wellness that set healthy leaders from toxic ones are purposeful life, quality connection to others, and positive self-regard and mastery, all of which are embedded within the three mini-triangle dimensions outlined above.

Taken together, the multidimensional model of servant leadership behavior discussed in this book provides a strong base for a holistic leadership development approach at the individual and organizational level. The servant leadership behavior scale (SLBS) can be employed as a guide to design a customized leadership development program and a gauge the effectiveness of the program in the pre- and post-intervention stages. With intentional and systematic development, servant leadership will operate like a breath of fresh air in the corporate ventilation system filled with a build-up of toxic emotions and unethical practices.

References

Arvey, R. D., Rotundo, M., Johnson, W., Zhang, Z., & McGue, M. (2006). The determinants of leadership role occupancy: Genetic and personality factors. *Leadership Quarterly, 17*, 1–20.

Avolio, B. J., & Vogelgesang, G. (2011). Beginnings matter in genuine leadership development. In S. E. Murphy & R. J. Reichard (Eds.), *Early development and leadership: Building the next generation of leaders* (pp. 179–204). New York: Psychology Press/Routledge.

Babiak, P., & Hare, R. D. (2007). *Snakes in suits: When psychopaths go to work*. New York: Harper Business.

Bennis, W. G. (1989). *On becoming a leader*. Reading: Addison-Wesley.

Bennis, W. G., & Thomas, R. J. (2002, September). Crucibles of leadership. *Harvard Business Review, 80*(9), 39–45.

Carlyle, T. (1888). *On heroes, hero-worship and the heroic in history*. New York: Fredrick A. Stokes & Brother.

Cawthorn, D. L. (1996). Leadership: The great man theory revisited. *Business Horizons, 39*(3), 1–4.

Day, D. V., Zaccaro, S. J., & Halpin, S. M. (Eds.). (2004). *Leaders development for transforming organizations: Growing leaders for tomorrow*. Mahwah: Lawrence Erlbaum Associates.

Fusaro, P. C., & Miller, R. M. (2002). *What went wrong at Enron*. Hoboken: Wiley.

George, B., Sims, P., McLean, A. N., & Mayer, D. (2007). Discovering your authentic leadership. *Harvard Business Review, 85*(2), 129–138.

Goodman, D. (2007). Leading with wounds: A liability or gift? *Journal of Religious Leadership, 6*(1), 39–69.

Hamilton, S., & Micklethwait, A. (2006). *Freed and corporate failure: The lessons from recent disasters*. New York: Palgrave Macmillan.

Hollander, E. P. (1995). Ethical challenges in the leader-follower relationship. *Business Ethics Quarterly, 5*(1), 55–65.

Hughes, R. L., Ginnett, R. C., & Curphy, G. J. (2005). *Leadership: Enhancing the lessons of experience* (5th ed.). Boston: McGraw-Hill.

Jung, C. G. (2000). *The collected works of C.G. Jung* (2nd ed.). Princeton: Princeton University Press.

Kets de Vries, M. F. R. (1994). The leadership mystique. *Academy of Management Executive, 8*(3), 73–92.

Kets de Vries, M., & Korotov, K. (2007). Creating transformational executive education programs. *Academy of Management Learning and Education, 6*(3), 375–387.

Kets de Vries, M. F. R., & Korotov, K. (2012). Transformational leadership development programs: Creating long-term sustainable change. In S. Snook, R. Khurana, & N. Nohria (Eds.), *The handbook for teaching leadership*. Boston: Harvard Business School Press.

Kiewitz, C., Restubog, S. L. D., Zagenczyk, T. J., Scott, K. L., Garcia, P. R. J. M., & Tang, R. L. (2012). Sins of the parents: Self-control as a buffer between supervisors' previous experience of family undermining and subordinates' perceptions of abusive supervision. *The Leadership Quarterly, 23*, 869–882.

King, M. L. (1963). *Letter from Birmingham Jail*. An unpublished letter.

McCauley, C. D., & Velsor, V. E. (Eds.). (2004). *The center for creative leadership handbook of leadership development* (2nd ed.). San Francisco: Jossey-Bass.

Murphy, S. E. (2011). Providing a foundation for leadership development. In S. E. Murphy & R. J. Reichard (Eds.), *Early development and leadership: Building the next generation of leaders* (pp. 3–37). New York: Psychology Press/Routledge.

Murphy, S. E., & Johnson, S. K. (2011). The benefits of a long-lens approach to leader development: Understanding the seeds of leadership. *Leadership Quarterly, 22*, 459–470.

Ney, P. G. (1987). Does verbal abuse leave deeper scars: A study of children and parents. *Canadian Journal of Psychiatry, 32*, 371–378.

Paunonen, S. V., Lönnqvist, J.-E., Verkasalo, M., Leikas, S., & Nissinen, V. (2006). Narcissism and emergent leadership in military cadets. *Leadership Quarterly, 17*, 475–486.

Price, T. L. (2005). Abuse, privilege, and the conditions of responsibility for leaders. In J. B. Ciulla, T. L. Price, & S. E. Murphy (Eds.), *The quest for moral leaders: Essays in leadership ethics*. Cheltenham: Edward Elgar.

Quick, J. C., Macik-Frey, M., & Cooper, C. L. (2007). Managerial dimensions of organizational health: The healthy leader at work. *Journal of Management Studies, 44*(2), 189–205.

Rosenthal, S. A., & Pittinsky, T. L. (2006). Narcissistic leadership. *The Leadership Quarterly, 17*(6), 617–633.

Rost, J. C. (1991). *Leadership for the twenty-first century*. New York: Praeger.

Schein, E. H. (1999). *The corporate culture survival guide: Sense and nonsense about culture change*. San Francisco: Jossey-Bass.

Shamir, B., & Eilam, G. (2005). "What's your story?" A life-stories approach to authentic leadership development. *The Leadership Quarterly, 16*(3), 395–417.

Sherry, S. B., Hewitt, P. L., Besser, A., Flett, G. L., & Klein, C. (2006). Machiavellianism, trait perfectionism, and perfectionistic self-presentation. *Personality and Individual Differences, 40*, 829–839.

Sinclair, A. (2007). *Leadership for the disillusioned: Moving beyond myths and heroes to leading that liberates*. Sydney: Allen & Unwin.

Stien, M. (2007). Oedipus Rex at Enron: Leadership, Oedipal struggles, and organizational collapse. *Human Resources, 60*(9), 1387–1410.

Sull, D. N., & Houlder, D. (2005, September). Do your commitments match your convictions? *Harvard Business Review, 83*(1), 82–91.

Tolstoy, L. (1869). *War and peace*. The Russian Messenger

U.S. Army. (2004). *Be, know, do: Leadership the army way: Adapted from the official army leadership manual*. San Francisco: Jossey-Bass.

Zhang, Z., Ilies, R., & Arvey, R. D. (2009). Beyond genetic explanations for leadership: The moderating role of the social environment. *Organizational Behavior and Human Decision Process, 110*, 118–128.

Appendix: Interviews Methods

Purpose of Interview

The qualitative data obtained from the interview were collected to generate themes pertinent to servant leadership. Specifically, direct quotations from the interviews of senior executives about their experiences, opinions, feelings, and knowledge on servant leadership constitute the qualitative data. The perceptions of the interview participants were particularly useful to generate in-depth understanding of the notion of servant leadership (Berg 1998). The interview data were also utilized in tandem with the preliminary literature review during the exploratory research phase to inform the development of the servant leadership measure (Bryman 1988).

Analytical Categories

All data documents were subdivided into the smallest segment of text (i.e. single-line text units) by way of coding schemes (Richards and Richards 1994). Strauss and Corbin (1990, p. 57) defined coding as a process by which "data are broken down, conceptualized, and put back together in new ways." The initial coding schemes or templates for the current study were developed *a priori* based on the review of the literature (Miles and Huberman 1984), and were refined and modified accordingly during the analytical process through exposure to the transcribed interview data (King 1994; Miller and Crabtree 1999b). This iterative process of content analysis and interpretation were continued until substantive analytical categories with clear theoretical underpinnings emerged.

Two levels of analytical categories were employed on the analytical process. The first level of analysis involved categorizing the comments according to the six dimensions of servant leadership, namely Voluntary Subordination, Authentic Self, Covenantal Relationship, Responsible Morality, Transcendental Spirituality, and Transforming Influence. *Voluntary Subordination* comments were categorized at the second level into *Being a Servant* and *Acts of Service*. *Authentic Self* comments were

© Springer International Publishing Switzerland 2015
S. Sendjaya, *Personal and Organizational Excellence through Servant Leadership*,
Management for Professionals, DOI 10.1007/978-3-319-16196-9

classified at the second level into *Humility, Integrity, Accountability, Security,* and *Vulnerability.* Comments concerning *Covenantal Relationship* were grouped at the second level into *Acceptance, Availability, Equality,* and *Collaboration. Responsible Morality* comments were categorized at the second level into *Moral Reasoning* and *Moral Action. Transcendental Spirituality* comments were grouped at the second level into *Religiousness, Interconnectedness, Sense of Mission,* and *Wholeness.* Finally, *Transforming Influence* comments were categorized at the second level into *Vision, Modeling, Mentoring, Trust,* and *Empowerment.* Overall, there were twenty two sub-dimensions of servant leadership into which the interview data were classified. The comments were applied at the second level of categorization for each variable to illustrate these two sub-dimensions.

Content analyses should include both quantitative and qualitative studies, in the sense that "qualitative analysis deals with the forms and antecedent-consequent patterns of form, while quantitative analysis deals with duration and frequency of form" (Smith 1975, p. 218). Accordingly, in the current study frequencies and percentage frequencies were calculated for the comments coded in each thematic category. A series of tally sheets was created to determine specific frequencies of relevant categories.

Validity and Reliability

The face validity of qualitative data was evident through the congruence between the data and the themes into which the data were categorized (Abrahamson 1983). Excerpts from the transcripts of interviews were provided to demonstrate that the theoretical frameworks and themes identified were grounded in the data. A minimum of three independent examples were cited for each interpretation whenever possible, following the procedure set by Berg (1998). Interrater reliability estimation is a recognized process in qualitative research useful for establishing a certain degree of accuracy in representation of meanings or categories developed by the researcher. Interrater reliability is achieved through the following process. Independent raters code interview comments without consultation with each other, calculate the statistical coefficients of agreement, and, whenever applicable, discuss reasons for disagreements, decide on a modified coding, and finally, code new comments to assess their agreement. The interrater reliability is estimated by calculating 'the number of coding agreements/number of coding agreements plus number of coding disagreements', as prescribed by Goodwin and Goodwin (1985, p. 7).

Coding agreements were achieved when two independent raters concurred on the classification of a comment. In the current study, themes of servant leadership identified were double coded by an independent rater to check the degree of consensus in the identification of the categories. A random sample of six transcripts, which accounts for 40 % of the total transcripts, was recoded independently. Miles and Huberman (1984) maintained that a .70 agreement rate is satisfactory for establishing interrater reliability. In this study, the statistical coefficient of agreement yielded a mean interrater reliability of .81, which exceeds the recommended rate.

Table 1 Sample for interviews

	Respondents	
	f	%[a]
Organization type		
For-profit	5	33
Not-for-profit	10	67
Industry		
Service	3	20
Banking	1	7
Software	1	7
Humanitarian	7	46
Research/Training	2	13
Professional association	1	7

[a]Percentages have been rounded

The Interview Sample

Purposive and snowball non-probability sampling techniques were used sequentially to determine the sample of the interviews (Minichiello et al. 1995; Tashakkori and Teddlie 1998). In relation to purposive sampling, seven respondents were initially identified as opinion leaders who advocated servant leadership both as a leadership ideal and practice, in accordance with the generative purpose of the interview. These interviewees were then asked to nominate their colleagues or others whom they knew fit the sample criteria of the current study. The snowball process was continued until adequate themes pertinent to servant leadership were identified, which in this case occurred at the 15th interview. Additional interviews would merely produce recurring themes and, hence, were considered unnecessary.

All in all, a total of 15 face-to-face in-depth interviews were conducted at the interviewee's place of business. Therefore, in view of the generative purpose of the interview, the small sample size (n = 15) was appropriate since the sampling did not have to be representative. Table 1 provides the frequency and percentage frequency distribution of the interview sample according to the organization type and industry.

Interview Process

The current study employed semi-structured interviews to create a guided and focused conversational journey out of the partnership between the interviewer and the interviewee (Miller and Crabtree 1999a). Since servant leadership was an emerging research area, the development of a flexible interview guide instead of rigidly structured interview schedule was more feasible and appropriate where the researcher has the flexibility to probe further and in line with the answers to the prepared questions (Miller and Crabtree 1999c, p. 19). In fact, the flexible interview guide was modified in line with respondents' responses in order to give them enough room to elaborate certain themes or discuss pertinent issues not covered in the predetermined questions, but which were considered significant (King 1994; Minichiello et al. 1995).

The sequence of the interview was carefully planned to maximize the generation of substantive insights on servant leadership from the participants. As such, the 'funnel technique', where researchers progress from the least threatening to most specific/sensitive questions, was employed (Schmitt and Klimoski 1991). Demographic questions concerning the respondents' age, education, training, duration of employment at the current organization and position, and number of subordinates were asked in the beginning as they were considered non-threatening questions, following the suggestion of Berg (1998) and Minichiello et al. (1995, p. 84). The interview progressed to generic, open-ended preliminary questions on general leadership qualities, responsibilities, and/or challenges in that sequential order, before asking specific questions on servant leadership.

The principal scheduled questions which followed revolved around the central focus of the study, namely themes pertinent to servant leadership. The perceived meaning of servant leadership was elicited from interviewees. In addition, scheduled and unscheduled probing questions were asked when deemed appropriate as follow-up questions to extract respondents' tacit understandings of servant leadership or to resolve contradictions which demanded more explanations (Minichiello et al. 1995; Schmitt and Klimoski 1991)

To obtain a better understanding of the context from where the respondents approach the topic (Rousseau and Fried 2001), respondents' perceptions of an ideal workplace and their personal purpose or passion were solicited based on examples from the literature (Delbecq 1999; Levering and Moskowitz 2001). Examples of servant leadership practices and comment on the outcomes of servant leadership in the organization were also asked whenever relevant. At the conclusion of the interview, interviewees were given the opportunity to contribute any other comments pertinent to the study that may not have been covered in the rest of the interview.

Prior to the interview, the researcher informed the interviewees that their anonymity would be preserved throughout the whole research process and in the final thesis. As results of the interview data were aggregated, neither the individual nor the organization were able to be identified. Selected background characteristics however were included for interest without violating anonymity. The relevant details included gender, organizational position, and industry classification.

Analysis of Interview Data

Content analysis of the transcribed interview data was facilitated by a qualitative analysis software program called NVivo (the latest version of NUD*IST, which stands for Non-numerical, Unstructured Data Indexing, Searching, and Theorizing). Holsti (1968, p. 608) defined content analysis as "any technique for making inferences by systematically and objectively identifying special characteristics of messages." NVivo was utilized to systematize, categorize, and code the interview data on the basis of specified characteristics of data to allow fluid exploration and interpretation of text (Richards 2002).

Table 2 Frequency and percentage frequency distributions of interview data in analytical categories

Theme	f	%[a]	I.R.[b]
Voluntary subordination			
Being a servant	8	42	.75
Acts of service	11	58	.80
Theme total	**19**	**100**	
Authentic self			
Humility	7	34	.80
Integrity	3	14	1.00
Accountability	3	14	1.00
Security	5	24	.80
Vulnerability	3	14	1.00
Theme total	**21**	**100**	
Covenantal relationship			
Acceptance	2	13	1.00
Availability	3	20	1.00
Equality	6	40	.71
Collaboration	4	27	1.00
Theme total	**15**	**100**	
Responsible morality			
Moral actions	2	40	1.00
Moral reasoning	3	60	1.00
Theme total	**5**	**100**	
Transcendental spirituality			
Religiousness	5	30	.80
Interconnectedness	3	18	1.00
Sense of mission	3	18	1.00
Wholeness	6	34	.75
Theme total	**17**	**100**	
Transforming influence			
Vision	5	22	.75
Modeling	7	31	.75
Mentoring	4	17	.75
Trust	3	13	1.00
Empowerment	4	17	.75
Theme total	**23**	**100**	

[a]Percentages have been rounded
[b]Interrater Reliability

The interview data were examined using the latent variables identified through the literature review as a theoretical framework for the analyses of the manifest data. The quasi-statistical approach (see King 1994) was employed to turn contextual data into quantitative data to allow the calculation of the frequencies and percentage frequencies of comments in each thematic category. Table 2 shows the frequencies, percentage frequencies, and the interrater reliabilities for each category.

References

Abrahamson, M. (1983). *Social research methods*. Englewood Cliffs: Prentice Hall.

Berg, B. L. (1998). *Qualitative research methods for the social sciences* (3rd ed.). Boston: Allyn and Bacon.

Bryman, A. (1988). *Quantity and quality in social research*. London: Unwin Hyman.

Delbecq, A. L. (1999). Christian spirituality and contemporary business leadership. *Journal of Organizational Change Management, 12*(4), 345–349.

Goodwin, L. D., & Goodwin, W. L. (1985). Statistical techniques in AERJ articles, 1979–1983: The preparation of graduate students to read the educational research literature. *Educational Researcher, 14*(2), 5–11.

Holsti, O. R. (1968). Content analysis. In G. Lindzey & E. Aaronson (Eds.), *The handbook of social psychology*. Reading: Addison-Wesley.

King, N. (1994). The qualitative research interview. In C. Cassell & G. Symon (Eds.), *Qualitative methods in organizational research: A practical guide* (pp. 14–36). Thousand Oaks: Sage Publications.

Levering, R., & Moskowitz, M. (2001, January 8). The 100 best companies to work for in America. *Fortune*.

Miles, M. B., & Huberman, A. M. (1984). *Qualitative data analysis: A sourcebook of new methods*. Beverly Hills: Sage.

Miller, W. L., & Crabtree, B. F. (1999a). Depth interviewing. In B. F. Crabtree & W. L. Miller (Eds.), *Doing qualitative research* (2nd ed., pp. 89–108). Thousand Oaks: Sage Publications.

Miller, W. L., & Crabtree, B. F. (1999b). Using codes and code manuals: A template organizing style of interpretation. In B. F. Crabtree & W. L. Miller (Eds.), *Doing qualitative research* (2nd ed., pp. 163–178). Thousand Oaks: Sage Publications.

Miller, W. L., & Crabtree, B. F. (1999c). Clinical research: A multimethod typology and qualitative roadmap. In B. F. Crabtree & W. L. Miller (Eds.), *Doing qualitative research* (2nd ed., pp. 3–30). Thousand Oaks: Sage.

Minichiello, V., Aroni, R., Timewell, E., & Alexander, L. (1995). *In-depth interviewing* (2nd ed.). Melbourne: Longman Cheshire.

Richards, L., & Richards, T. (1994). Using computers in qualitative analysis. In N. K. Denzin & Y. S. Lincoln (Eds.), *Handbook of qualitative research* (pp. 445–462). Thousand Oaks: Sage.

Richards, L. (2002). *Introducing NVivo: A workshop handbook*. Doncaster: QSR International.

Rousseau, D. M., & Fried, Y. (2001). Location, location, location: Contextualizing organizational research. *Journal of Organizational Behavior, 22*, 1–13.

Schmitt, N. W., & Klimoski, R. J. (1991). *Research methods in human resource management*. Cincinnati: South-Western Publishing.

Smith, H. W. (1975). *Strategies of social research*. Englewood Cliffs: Prentice Hall.

Strauss, A., & Corbin, J. (1990). *Basics of qualitative research: Grounded theory procedures and techniques*. Newbury Park: Sage Publications.

Tashakkori, A., & Teddlie, C. (1998). *Mixed methodology*. Thousand Oaks: Sage.

CPSIA information can be obtained
at www.ICGtesting.com
Printed in the USA
LVOW13*1534050317

526190LV00008B/377/P